Tunisian Crochet
FOR Beginners

Tunisian Crochet
FOR Beginners

Patterns for beautifully textured
accessories, decorations, blankets,
and more

Laura Strutt

CICO BOOKS
LONDON NEW YORK

**For Ethan Wolf & Elkie Raven—
no matter what**

Published in 2024 by CICO Books
an imprint of Ryland Peters & Small Ltd
341 E 116th St, New York, NY 10029

www.rylandpeters.com

10 9 8 7 6 5 4 3 2 1

Text © Laura Strutt 2024
Design, illustration, and photography
© CICO Books 2024

A CIP catalog record for this book is available from
the Library of Congress.

ISBN: 978 1 80065 381 8

Printed in China

Editor: Marie Clayton
Pattern checker: Carol Ibbetson
Designer: Alison Fenton
Photographer: James Gardiner
Equipment photography on page 9: Martin Norris
Stylist: Nel Haynes
Illustrators: Cathy Brear (pages 11—Holding the
hook and yarn, 12—Parts of the stitch, 13—Return
pass, 14–16, 18–19, 21–25) and Stephen Dew
(pages 10, 11—Making a slip knot and yarn round
hook, 12–13—Chain, 13—Foundation, 17—
Fastening off, 20—Joining yarn, 26–31)

In-house editor: Jenny Dye
Art director: Sally Powell
Creative director: Leslie Harrington
Head of production: Patricia Harrington
Publishing manager: Carmel Edmonds

Contents

Introduction

I have always been drawn to the distinctive woven finish of Tunisian crochet. Despite one of its most used stitches—Tunisian Simple Stitch—looking like intricate yarn work, no one was more delighted than me when I discovered that it lived up to its name and was surprisingly quick and easy to master. With traits of both knitting and crochet, this is an ideal craft whether you have experience working with knitting needles or crochet hooks... or if you are new to yarn crafts!

Tunisian crochet is a type of crochet that works with multiple stitches on the hook at a time. The stitches are worked back and forth in rows, much like knitting, and create some of the most wonderful textured fabrics. These dense, highly textured stitches are commonly used for cozy blankets and sumptuous wraps, but since they are often robust and hard-wearing, they are also a great choice for dishcloths, placemats, and home accessories.

In this collection, I wanted to showcase the range of projects that can be made using this craft, from light and airy shawls to chunky wintertime accessories and striking décor pieces. I have used a wide selection of yarns to achieve both luxe finishes alongside more durable, everyday items.

I thoroughly enjoyed designing and making the projects in this book and I hope this sets you off on your journey of discovery with Tunisian crochet!

Before you begin

If you are new to Tunisian crochet, or if you come across a technique you don't understand, please check out the Techniques section on pages 10–31 and the Abbreviations on page 31. On page 8, you'll also find a guide to the basic tools you'll need. Each of the projects has a skill rating, from Very Easy (one circle) to Easy (two circles) and Intermediate (three circles). Start with the Very Easy patterns, then move on to the next two levels once you have got to know the basic techniques.

Tools

Here you'll find the basic tools you will need for all the projects in this book.

Tunisian crochet hooks

Tunisian crochet hooks are longer than traditional crochet hooks so that they can hold on to a greater number of stitches. They are either a solid hook with an extended handle or a hook with a flexible cable. Both straight and cable Tunisian hooks feature a stopper on the end to prevent the stitches from sliding off. Both types can be used for crocheting patterns that are worked flat (as the projects are in this book). However, if you are working on a very large project, you may want to opt for a hook with a cable as it can accommodate a greater number of stitches. A hook with a cable can also feel easier on your hands and wrists as you aren't holding the full weight of the project as you work.

You may also come across Tunisian crochet hooks with a hook at either end. These are often used for more complex techniques such as working in the round or on both sides. These techniques are not featured in this book.

As with traditional crochet hooks, you will find ones made from a range of materials including wood, metal, bamboo, and acrylic. The type of hook you use is usually down to personal preference. For example, wood and bamboo hooks are lighter and warmer to hold; however, the yarn may not glide as smoothly as it does on a metal hook. Acrylic hooks are often a great beginner option as they are smooth to use, light and usually less expensive. You may like to try a few different styles and could find that you have different hook preferences for different yarns and styles of projects.

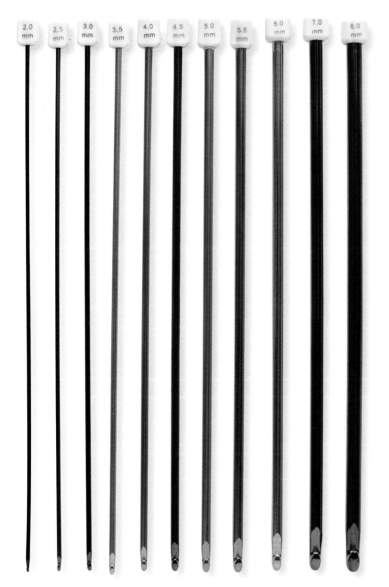

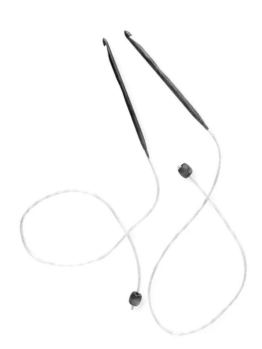

Tape measure

You will need one of these for checking your gauge (tension, see page 26) and for blocking your projects to the finished size (see page 28).

Locking or split-ring stitch markers

Locking or split-ring markers are used to identify the start of a round and to help you keep track of the pattern.

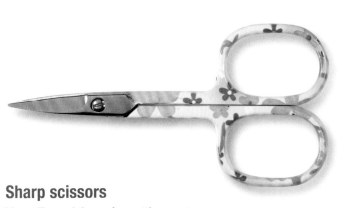

Sharp scissors

You will need these for cutting yarn after finishing a piece and when sewing up. It is tempting to break yarn with your hands, but this can pull the stitches out of shape.

Yarn needle

These come in various sizes, but all have large eyes for easy threading of yarn, and a blunt end that will not split the stitches when you are sewing up your work.

Pins

Long rustproof, glass-headed, or T-headed quilter's pins can be used to pin crocheted pieces together for sewing up. Bright-colored tops make it easy to spot the pins against the crocheted fabric so you don't leave any behind!

Techniques

This section guides you through all the crochet and finishing techniques you will need to make the projects in this book. It includes Tunisian crochet stitches that create its distinctive textures, as well as some traditional crochet techniques that are also used in Tunisian crochet (see pages 11, 12, and 27). If you're new to traditional crochet or Tunisian crochet, practice the skills covered in this section before you start on a project. Keep the loops of your stitches loose—you can work on creating an even gauge (see page 26) across the fabric as you develop your skills.

Essential skills

Holding the yarn

Below is the most common way to hold the yarn, but yarn holds can be different depending on your personal preference. Hold the yarn in the way that's most comfortable for you and allows you to maintain gauge (tension) in the yarn—this usually involves wrapping the yarn around a few of your fingers.

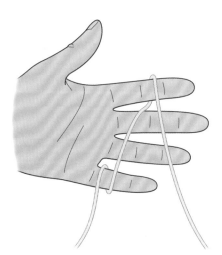
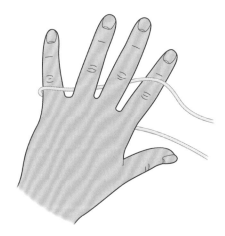

1. Pick up the yarn with your little finger in the opposite hand to your hook, with your palm facing upward and with the short end in front. Turn your hand to face downward, with the yarn on top of your index finger and under the other two fingers and wrapped right around the little finger, as shown above.

2. Turn your hand to face you, ready to hold the work in your middle finger and thumb. Keeping your index finger only at a slight curve, hold the work or the slip knot using the same hand, between your middle finger and your thumb and just below the crochet hook and loop/s on the hook.

Holding the hook and yarn while crocheting

In standard crochet, it is common to hold the hook in either a knife hold or a pen hold. Since you are holding a lot of stitches at a time and using a longer hook, the knife hold is required for Tunisian crochet. When your hand is positioned over the hook, all of your fingers are in contact with the hook, making it easier to maintain the gauge (tension) of the stitches and the multiple loops on the hook. The knife hold means that your palm has the hook running against it and your ring and pinky finger can hold the hook. Your thumb and middle finger make a pinch over the hook and move the Tunisian crochet fabric and loops along. Meanwhile, as you work, your index finger can be placed on the hook or help make the next stitch.

In your left hand, keep your index finger, with the yarn draped over it, at a slight curve, and hold your work (or the slip knot) using the same hand, between your middle finger and your thumb and just below the hook. As you

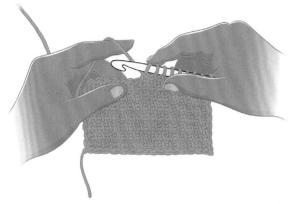

draw the loop through the hook, release the yarn on the index finger to allow the loop to stay loose on the hook. If you tense your index finger, the yarn will become too tight and pull the loop on the hook too tight for you to draw the yarn through.

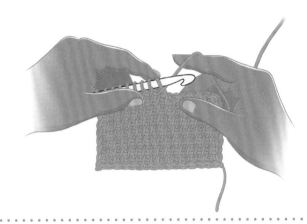

Holding the hook and yarn for left-handers

Some left-handers learn to crochet like right-handers, but others learn with everything reversed—with the hook in the left hand and the yarn in the right.

Making a slip knot

A slip knot is the loop that you put onto the hook to start any stitch.

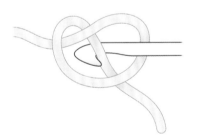 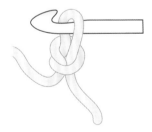

1. In one hand hold the circle at the top where the yarn crosses, and let the tail drop down at the back so that it falls across the center of the loop. With your free hand or the tip of a crochet hook, pull a loop through the circle.

2. Put the hook into the loop and pull gently so that it forms a loose loop on the hook.

Yarn over hook (yoh)

To create a stitch, catch the yarn from behind with the hook pointing upward. As you gently pull the yarn through the loop on the hook, turn the hook so it faces downward and slide the yarn through the loop. The loop on the hook should be kept loose enough for the hook to slide through easily.

Basic Tunisian crochet stitches

Stitches in Tunisian crochet have a slightly different look to standard crochet stitches. The top part of each stitch has two horizontal bars, similar to a standard crochet stitch, but below this each stitch has two vertical bars, one at the front and one at the back. Follow the instructions for each stitch to know where to insert the hook.

Parts of the stitch

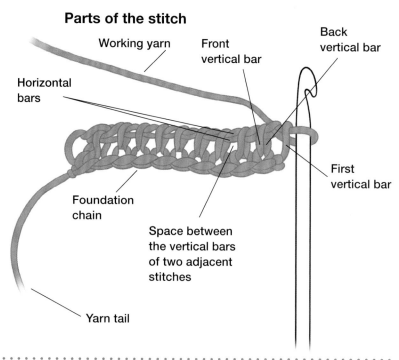

Working yarn

Front vertical bar

Back vertical bar

Horizontal bars

First vertical bar

Foundation chain

Space between the vertical bars of two adjacent stitches

Yarn tail

Chain

Chains are the basis of all Tunisian and standard crochet; you need to make a length of chains to be able to make the first row or round of any other stitch. Practicing making chains will also give you the chance to get used to holding the hook and the yarn correctly.

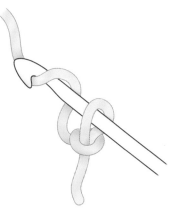

1. Using the hook, wrap the yarn over the hook ready to pull it through the loop on the hook.

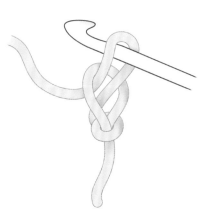

2. Pull through, creating a new loop on the hook. Continue in this way to create a chain of the required length.

Front of chain
The front of the chain (the right side) is the smooth side: each chain makes a little "V."

Back of chain
The back of the chain (the wrong side) is more bumpy, with little ridges.

Counting chains

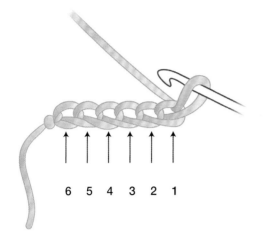

6 5 4 3 2 1

To count chains in a foundation chain, lay the chain out on a flat surface with the right side facing you and count each "V" as one chain. Always count chains from the front of the chain (the end nearest to the hook) and do not count the loop on the hook as one chain.

Foundation

Tunisian crochet projects will usually begin with a foundation row. This is the first row of Tunisian stitches that are worked into a length of chain stitches. It will make up the lower edge of the Tunisian crochet fabric.

1. Make the number of chain stated in the pattern.

2. Starting in the second chain from the hook, insert the hook from front to back through the back loop on the chain. Yarn over hook and pull through, to add a new loop on the hook. Repeat to the end of the row of chain stitches.

Return pass

Tunisian crochet is worked in two stages. The first is the Forward Pass (worked from right to left), where the stitches are made and placed on the hook. The second stage is the Return Pass which is worked from left to right, where the stitches are each worked off the hook in turn, leaving only one stitch (loop) on the hook.

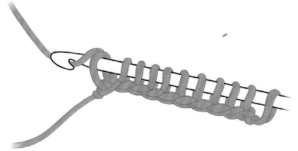

1. Yarn over hook.

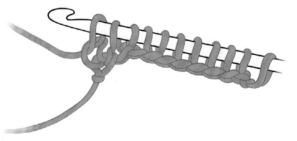

2. Draw through the first stitch.

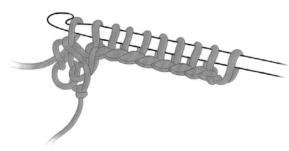

3. Yarn over hook, draw through the next two stitches on the hook.

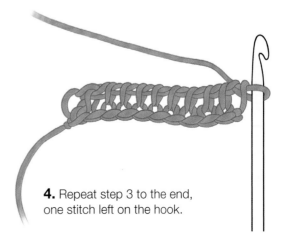

4. Repeat step 3 to the end, one stitch left on the hook.

Tunisian Simple Stitch (TSS)

This stitch is worked under only the front vertical bar each time.

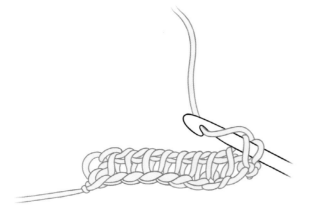

1. Skip the first vertical bar, insert the hook from right to left under the second vertical bar, yarn over hook.

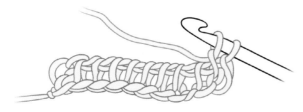

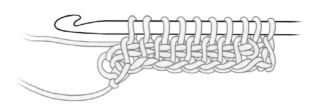

2. Draw through and leave the loop on the hook.

3. Repeat, pulling up a loop in the vertical bar of the next stitch along each time, to one stitch before the end.

End stitch

This stitch is worked under both the front and back vertical bars of the final stitch.

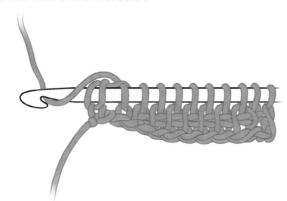

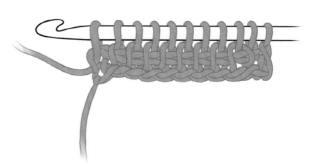

1. Rotate the work and insert the hook under the last vertical bar and the bar that lies directly behind it (two additional bars on the hook). Yarn over hook.

2. Draw through to finish.

Tunisian Knit Stitch (TKS)

This stitch is worked in between the front and back vertical bar each time.

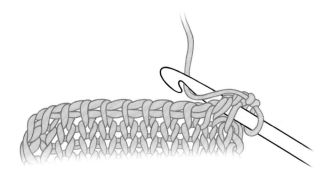

1. Skip the first vertical bar, insert the hook from front to back between the front and back vertical bars of the next stitch. Yarn over hook.

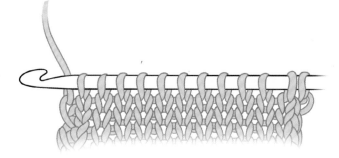

2. Draw through and leave the loop on the hook.

3. Repeat, inserting the hook between the front and back vertical bars of the next stitch along and pulling up a loop each time, to the end.

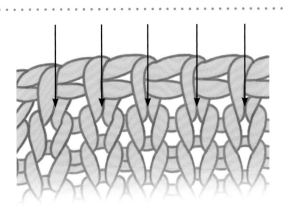

These arrows show where to insert the hook in each Tunisian Knit Stitch.

Tunisian Purl Stitch (TPS)

This stitch is worked under only the front vertical bar each time.

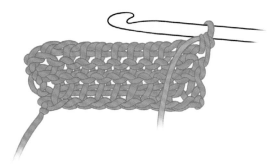

1. Skip the first vertical bar, bring the yarn to the front of the work.

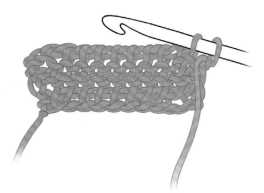

2. Insert the hook from right to left under the next vertical bar.

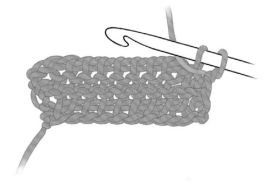

3. Take the yarn to the back of the work.

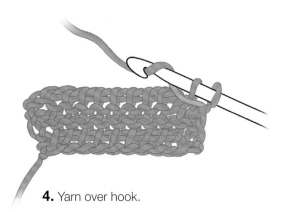

4. Yarn over hook.

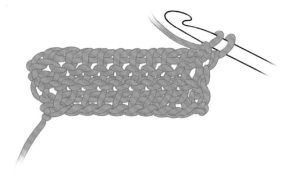

5. Draw through and leave the loop on the hook.

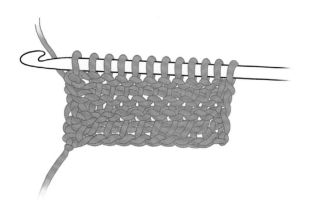

6. Repeat in the next vertical bar along each time to the end.

Bind (cast) off

This stitch is worked under only the front vertical bar each time.

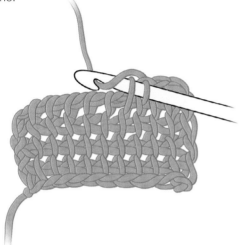

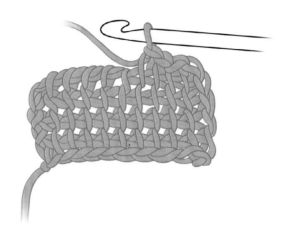

1. Skip the first vertical bar, insert the hook under the next vertical bar. Yarn over hook.

2. Draw through BOTH loops on the hook.

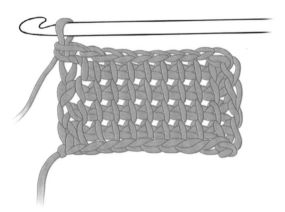

3. Repeat to the end. Cut the yarn and draw through the last loop to fasten off.

Decreasing

Decreasing 1 stitch (2TSStog)
This stitch is worked under only the front vertical bars each time.

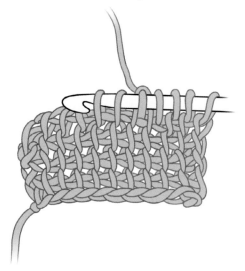

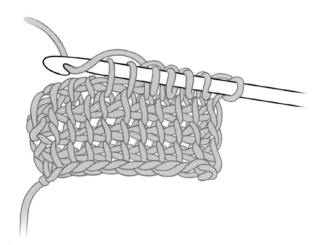

1. Insert the hook under the next two vertical bars.

2. Yarn over hook.

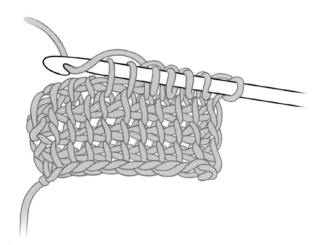

3. Draw through to leave a loop and decrease by one stitch.

Decreasing 2 stitches (3TSStog)

This stitch is worked under only the front vertical bars each time.

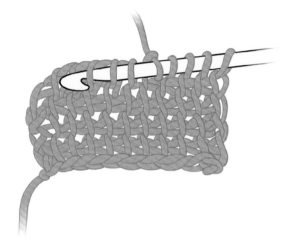

1. Insert the hook under the next three vertical bars.

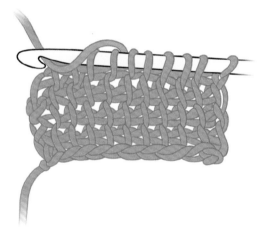

2. Yarn over hook.

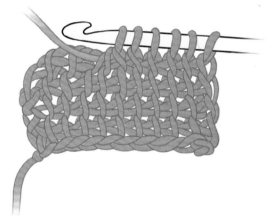

3. Draw through to leave a loop and decrease by two stitches.

Increasing in Tunisian Simple Stitch (M1TSS)

This stitch is worked into the space between the vertical bars of two adjacent stitches.

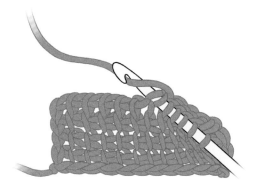

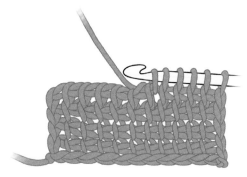

1. Insert the hook from the front to the back of the work, in the space between two vertical bars. Yarn over hook.

2. Draw through and leave on the hook as a new stitch.

Joining yarn at the end of a row or round

You can use this technique when changing color, or when joining in a new ball of yarn as one runs out.

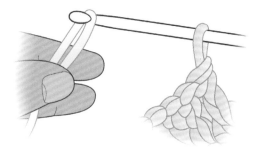

1. Keep the loop of the old yarn on the hook. Drop the tail and catch a loop of the strand of the new yarn with the crochet hook.

2. Draw the new yarn through the loop on the hook, keeping the old loop drawn tight and continue as instructed in the pattern.

Joining in new yarn after fastening off

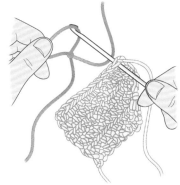

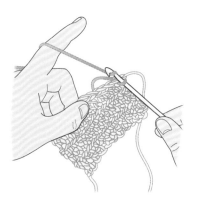

1. Fasten off the old color (see page 17). Make a slip knot with the new color (see page 11). Insert the hook into the stitch at the beginning of the next row, then through the slip knot.

2. Draw the loop of the slip knot through to the front of the work. Carry on working using the new color, following the instructions in the pattern.

Special stitches

Tunisian Front Post Treble Crochet (TFPTC)

This is worked in a similar way to a normal crochet front post stitch, so around the strands of the stitch below.

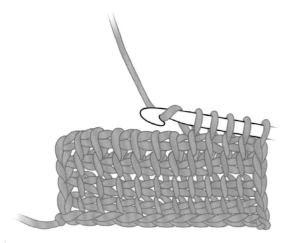

1. Yarn over hook.

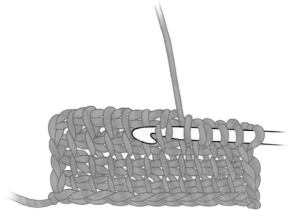

2. Insert the hook under both strands of the stitch in the row below.

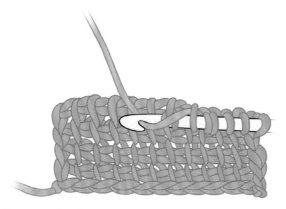

3. Yarn over hook.

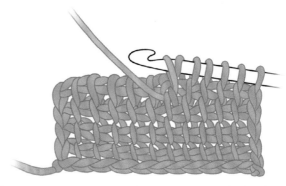

4. Pull through—there will be two loops on the hook from this stitch.

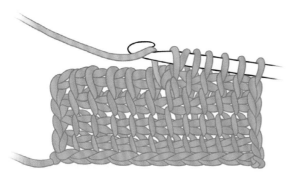

5. Yarn over hook again.

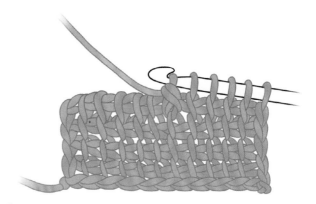

6. Pull through both loops on the hook.

Tunisian Smock Stitch

Tunisian Smock Stitch is a two stitch pattern repeated over two rows. The smock stitch design is created by alternating yarn under—as opposed to a yarn over—and Tunisian Simple Stitch 2 Together across the row.

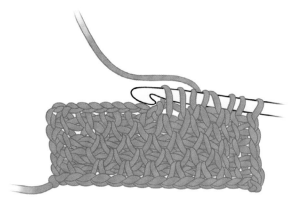

1. Insert the hook under the next two vertical bars.

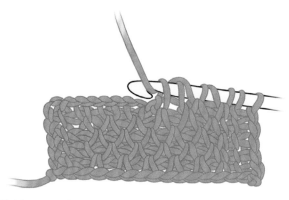

2. Yarn over hook as usual.

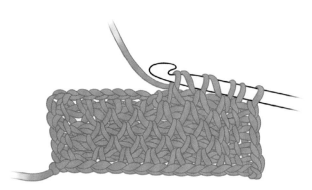

3. Draw through the two strands on the hook to leave a loop on the hook.

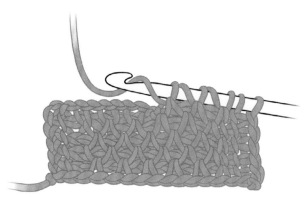

4. Bring the yarn under the hook to the front of the work, and then bring it back over the hook to create the yarn under.

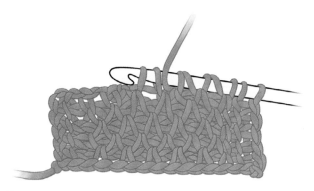

5. With the yarn under held in place, insert the hook under the next two vertical bars to continue.

Yarn Over (YO)

With this technique you take the yarn over the hook before working the stitch, which creates an extra loop of yarn over the hook. This can either be dropped for Drop Stitch, or wrapped around the base of following stitches for Wrap Stitch.

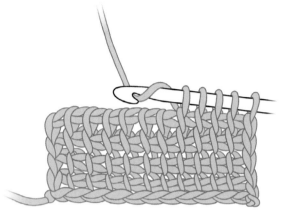

1. Yarn over hook.

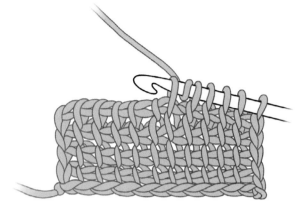

2. Insert the hook under the next vertical bar.

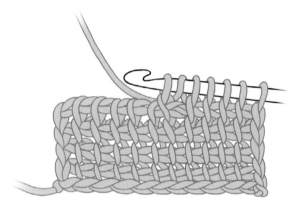

3. Yarn over hook, and draw through one strand to leave a loop on the hook.

Drop Stitch Return Pass with YO

Drop stitches are worked using a sized-up hook and with yarn overs that are dropped on the return pass to create a lacy, open fabric.

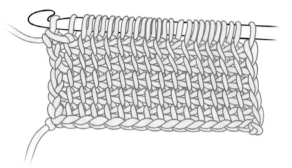

1. Work the Return Pass to the yarn over.

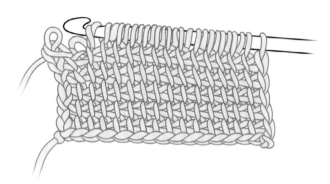

2. Slide the current stitch off and then drop the yarn over off the hook.

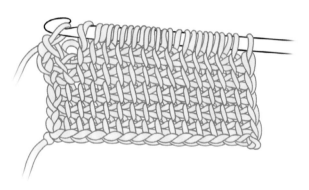

3. Return the current stitch to the hook.

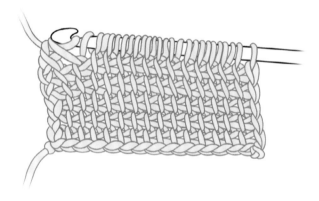

4. Yarn over hook, and draw through two strands to leave a loop on the hook.

Wrap Stitch

This stitch is created by bringing the yarn over the hook before working the stitch, which creates an extra loop of yarn over the hook, working the number of stitches stated and then lifting the yarn over across over the stitches to wrap them.

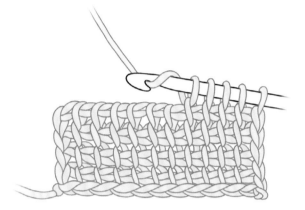

1. Work to the stitches to be wrapped. Yarn over hook.

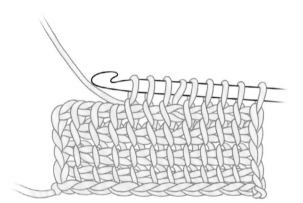

2. Work number of stitches to be wrapped—here it is three stitches.

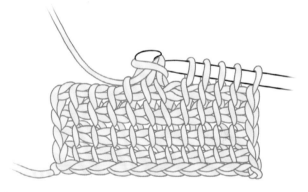

3. Lift the yarn over across over the worked stitches.

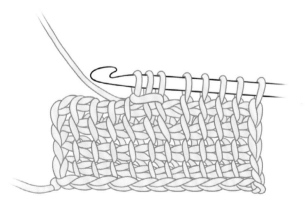

4. The yarn over wraps the base of the stitches.

How to measure a gauge (tension) square

Make a number of chains that measure to approximately 5–6in (13–15cm) using the hook and the yarn recommended in the pattern. Using the stitch given in the gauge guide at the beginning of the pattern, make enough rows to form a square and then fasten off. The stitches shown in this illustration are traditional crochet stitches, but the same method applies to Tunisian crochet.

Take a tape measure or ruler, place it across your crocheted piece horizontally, and mark off an area of 4in (10cm) with pin markers. Count the number of stitches across 4in (10cm), then take the tape measure/ruler and place it vertically and count the number of rows across 4in (10cm). Compare the number of stitches and rows you have counted to the gauge guide. If your rows and stitches measure the same as the guide, use this size hook and yarn to achieve the same gauge and measurements in the pattern. If you have more stitches, then your gauge is tighter than the sample and you need to use a larger crochet hook; if you have fewer stitches, then your gauge is looser and you'll need to use a smaller hook. Make gauge squares using different size hooks until you have reached the same gauge as the guide and then use this hook to make the project.

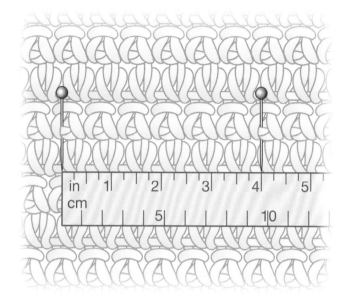

Other techniques

These traditional crochet techniques are used in some of the projects in this book.

Magic ring

This is a useful starting technique if you do not want a visible hole in the center of your round. Loop the yarn around your finger, insert the hook through the ring, yarn over hook, pull through the ring to make the first chain. Work the number of stitches required into the ring and then pull the end to tighten the center ring and close the hole.

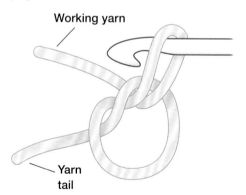

Working yarn

Yarn tail

Slip stitch (sl st)

A slip stitch doesn't create any height and is often used as the last stitch to create a smooth and even round or row.

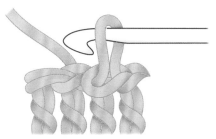

1. To make a slip stitch: first put the hook through the work, yarn over hook.

2. Pull the yarn through both the work and through the loop on the hook at the same time, so you will have one loop on the hook.

Single crochet (sc)

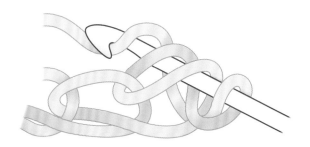

1. Insert the hook into your work, yarn over hook, and pull the yarn through the work only. You will then have two loops on the hook.

2. Yarn over hook again and pull through the two loops on the hook. You will then have one loop on the hook.

Single crochet 2 stitches together (sc2tog)

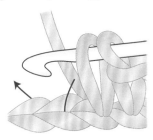

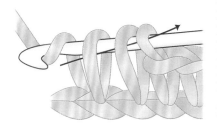

1. Insert the hook into your work, yarn over hook and pull the yarn through the work (two loops on hook). Insert the hook in next stitch, yarn over hook, and pull the yarn through.

2. Yarn over hook again and pull through all three loops on the hook. You will then have one loop on the hook.

Working into back loop of stitch (BLO)

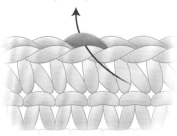

To work into the back loop of the stitch, insert the hook between the front and the back loop, picking up the back loop from the front of the work.

Finishing your projects

Weaving in yarn ends

It is important to weave in the tail ends of the yarn so that they are secure and your crochet won't unravel. Thread a yarn needle with the tail end of yarn. On the wrong side, take the needle through the crochet one stitch down on the edge, then take it through the stitches, working in a gentle zig-zag. Work through four or five stitches then return in the opposite direction. Remove the needle, pull the crochet gently to stretch it and trim the end.

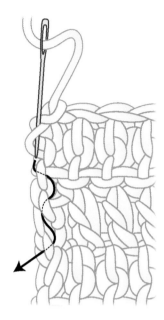

Blocking

Tunisian crochet is prone to curling and there are several ways to help prevent this. Going up a few hook sizes compared to the recommended crochet hook on the ball band will help. Once the project is completed you may also like to block the work to remove the curling. The stitches shown here are traditional crochet stitches, but the same method is used for blocking Tunisian crochet.

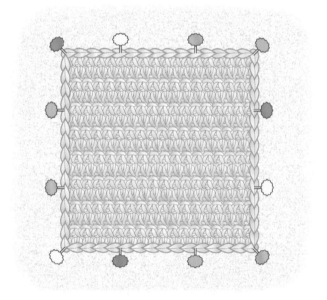

Blocking is the process of pinning out the work to the desired shape and measurements and applying steam or water which, once dried, will help the fibers to lay in the preferred way. When it comes to blocking, the wet method offers great results. To do this, pin the crochet into place to your desired shape and finished measurements on an ironing board or some soft foam mats (such as the ones sold as children's play mats). Spray the crochet with water and leave it to dry completely before unpinning and removing from the board or mats. Alternatively, instead of spraying with water you can use a blast of steam from an iron to help shape the pinned-out pieces. Be careful when applying steam—although it is great for natural fibers it can permanently damage blended or manmade fibers such as acrylic. Always check the yarn band and follow the care instructions for the yarn you are using.

With wear, use or simply over time, you may find that your projects start curling again. You will need to reblock to return them to your preferred shape. This can be done after the items are carefully hand-washed.

Seams

Mattress stitch seam

You can either gently pull the sewn stitches taut but have them visible, as shown, or you can pull them completely tight so that they disappear.

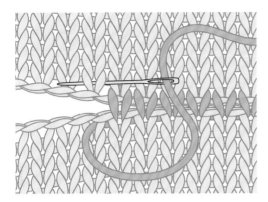

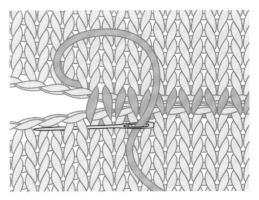

1. Right-sides up, lay the two edges to be joined side by side. Thread a yarn needle with a long length of yarn. Secure the yarn on the back of the lower piece, then bring the needle up through the middle of the first whole stitch in that piece. *Take the needle under both loops of the first whole stitch on the upper piece, so that it comes to the front between the first and second stitches.

2. Go back into the lower piece and take the needle through to the back where it first came out, and then bring it back to the front in the middle of the next stitch along. Pull the yarn through. Take the needle under both loops of the next whole stitch on the upper piece. Repeat from * to sew along the seam.

Single crochet and slip stitch seams

With a single crochet seam you join two pieces together using a crochet hook and working a single crochet stitch through both pieces, instead of sewing them together with a tail of yarn and a yarn sewing needle. This makes a quick and strong seam and gives a slightly raised finish to the edging. For a less raised seam, follow the same basic technique, but work each stitch in slip stitch rather than single crochet.

1. Start by lining up the two pieces with wrong sides together. Insert the hook in the top two loops of the stitch of the first piece, then into the corresponding stitch on the second piece.

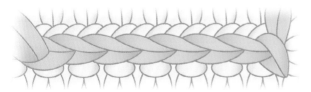

2. Complete the single crochet stitch as normal and continue on the next stitches as directed in the pattern. This gives a raised effect if the single crochet stitches are made on the right side of the work.

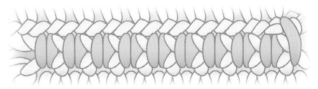

3. You can work with the wrong side of the work facing (with the pieces right-sides facing) if you don't want this effect and it still creates a good strong join.

Running stitch

Bring the needle to the surface of the fabric and take it back down to the left of the entry point, to create a straight stitch. Bring the needle back to the surface a stitch length away from the last stitch and return through the fabric as before. Continue to create stitches of equal length.

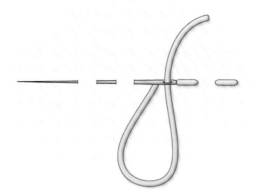

Adding tassels

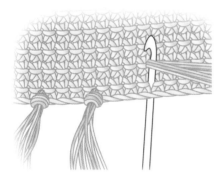

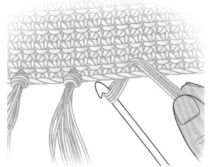

1. Cut strands of yarn to the length given in the pattern. Take one or more strands and fold in half. With the right side of the project facing, insert a crochet hook in one of the edge stitches from the wrong side. Catch the bunch of strands with the hook at the fold point.

2. Draw all the loops through the stitch.

3. Pull through to make a big loop and, using your fingers, pull the tails of the bunch of strands through the loop.

4. Pull on the tails to tighten the loop firmly to secure the tassel.

Sewing on a button

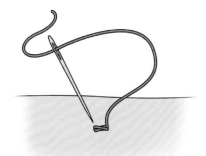

1. Push the needle up from the back of the crochet and sew a few small stitches in the position of the button.

2. Bring the needle up through one of the button's holes, holding the button with the other hand. Push the needle down through the second hole and the crochet. Bring it back up through the fabric and then the first hole. Repeat five or six times. Make sure you go up and down through the button's holes so the yarn doesn't loop around the side of the button. If your button has four holes, use all four of them to make either a cross or parallel pattern. Then wrap the yarn around the threads beneath the button a few times, pulling the thread tight. Finish with a few small stitches on the back of the crochet and trim the yarn.

Crochet term conversion chart

Crochet stitches are worked in the same way in both the USA and the UK, but the stitch names and terms are not the same. On the right is a list of the US terms used in this book, and the equivalent UK terms.

US term	UK term
single crochet (sc)	double crochet (dc)
gauge	tension
yarn over hook (yoh)	yarn round hook (yrh)

Abbreviations

BLO	back loop only	**TFPTC**	Tunisian Front Post Treble Crochet
ch	chain	**TKS**	Tunisian Knit Stitch
cont	continu(e)ing	**TPS**	Tunisian Purl Stitch
inc	increase: work 2 single crochet in next stitch	**TSS**	Tunisian Simple Stitch
		2TSStog	decrease by 1 stitch in Tunisian Simple Stitch
M1TSS	make one stitch in Tunisian Simple Stitch	**3TSStog**	decrease by 2 stitches in Tunisian Simple Stitch
opp	opposite		
PM	place marker	**WS**	wrong side
rep	repeat	**YO**	yarn over
RS	right side	**yoh**	yarn over hook
sc	single crochet	**YU**	yarn under
sc2tog	single crochet 2 stitches together	*****	repeat sequence from * the number of times stated
sl st	slip stitch		
sp	space	**[ ]**	repeat sequence between square brackets the number of times stated
st(s)	stitches		

Chapter 1

Hats, Scarves & Shawls

Ear Warmer Headband

Slip on this cozy headband to beat the wind and chills. Worked in a Tunisian Knit Stitch and folded double, this project is quick to make and a great alternative to a woolly hat when the seasons change.

SKILL RATING: ●

YARN AND MATERIALS

Sirdar Hayfield Bonus Extra Value DK (100% acrylic) light worsted (DK) weight yarn, approx 306yd (280m) per 3½oz (100g) ball
    1 ball of Lagoon Blue shade 607

HOOK AND EQUIPMENT

US size J-10 (6mm) Tunisian crochet hook

Yarn needle

FINISHED MEASUREMENTS

4 x 9½in (10 x 24cm) when laid flat

GAUGE (TENSION)

7 sts x 8 rows = 2 x 2in (5 x 5cm) in Tunisian Knit Stitch using a US size J-10 (6mm) hook, after blocking.

ABBREVIATIONS

See page 31.

STITCH USED

Tunisian Knit Stitch (TKS) (see page 15)

- -

Make it yours

This ear warmer is made from a rectangle that is folded in half and seamed. You can create your own custom size by making the rectangle larger for bigger sizes or smaller for a child size.

The hook size recommendation on the yarn was US size G-6 (4mm), but I used a US size J-10 (6mm).

- -

Headband

Foundation chain and forward pass: Ch32, starting in second ch from hook, working into back bumps of chain, pick up 31 sts for foundation row. (*32 loops on hook, 32 sts*)
Return pass: Yoh, draw through first st, *yoh, draw through next 2 sts on hook; rep from * to end.
(*1 st on hook*)
Row 1 (forward pass): Starting in the second st, TKS to last vertical bar, work end st. (*32 sts*)
Work Return Pass.
Rep Row 1 and the Return Pass, maintaining st count on Forward Pass, until work measures 20in (50.5cm) in length.
On next Forward Pass row, bind (cast) off.
Leave a long tail to sew together.

Making up and finishing

Weave in all ends and block flat to the desired measurements (see page 28).
Thread the yarn end onto a yarn needle. Align the two longer edges of the headband and, using mattress stitch, sew together along the length (see page 29).
Fasten off at the end and, without cutting the yarn tail, align the two short ends with the center seam of the tube running around the outer surface. Work across the ends to sew together, ensuring that the stitches are worked through all the layers. Fasten off, don't cut the yarn. Rotate so that the long seam lies to the inside of the headband.
Fold the join section to make a concertina by bringing the outer edges in toward the center, then sew to secure working the stitches through all the folds. Weave in all yarn ends.
Working from the remaining yarn in the ball—or a contrast shade if you prefer—take the yarn ends and begin neatly wrapping them around the center of the band over the join section. Continue wrapping until the entire section is covered. Fasten off and weave in all ends (see page 28).

Bold Chunky Scarf

Nothing quite beats that feeling of wrapping yourself up in a long chunky scarf. This design, worked in Tunisian Simple Stitch, features stripes and bold colors on the ends with a neutral tone in the center for a dramatic finish when draped around your neck.

SKILL RATING: ●

YARN AND MATERIALS

Stylecraft Special Chunky (100% acrylic) bulky (chunky) weight, approx 157yd (144m) per 3½oz (100g) ball
1 ball each of:
   Mustard shade 1823 (A)
   Silver shade 1203 (B)
   Storm Blue shade 1722 (C)

HOOK AND EQUIPMENT

US size L-11 (8mm) Tunisian crochet hook

Yarn needle

FINISHED MEASUREMENTS

7¾in (19.5cm) wide

76¼in (194cm) long

GAUGE (TENSION)

11 sts x 9 rows = 4 x 4in (10 x 10cm) in Tunisian Simple Stitch using an US size L-11 (8mm) hook, after blocking.

ABBREVIATIONS

See page 31.

STITCH USED

Tunisian Simple Stitch (TSS) (see page 14)

Scarf

Foundation chain and forward pass: Using A, ch21, starting in second ch from hook, working into back bumps of chain, pick up 20 sts for foundation row. *(21 loops on hook, 21 sts)*

Return pass 1: Yoh, draw through first st, *yoh, draw through next 2 sts on hook; rep from * to end. *(1 st on hook)*

Row 1: Starting in the second st, TSS to last vertical bar, work end st. *(21 sts)*
Work Return Pass 1.

Rows 2–48: Rep Row 1 and the Return Pass 1 a further 47 times.

Row 49: Starting in the second st, TSS to last vertical bar, work end st.

Return pass 2: Yoh, draw through first st, *yoh, draw through next 2 sts on hook; rep from * to last 2 sts on hook, join in B, yoh, draw through last 2 sts on hook. *(1 st on hook in B)*
Fasten off A.

Rows 50–128: Using B, rep Row 1 and the Return Pass 1 a total of 79 times.

Row 129: Using B starting in the second st, TSS to last vertical bar, work end st.

Return pass 3: Yoh, draw through first st, *yoh, draw through next 2 sts on hook; rep from * to last 2 sts on hook, join in C, yoh, draw through last 2 sts on hook. *(1 st on hook in C)*
Fasten off B.

Rows 130 and 131: Using C, rep Row 1 and the Return Pass 1 twice.

Row 132: Using C, starting in the second st, TSS to last vertical bar, work end st.
Work Return Pass 2, changing to B.
Fasten off C.

Rows 133 and 134: Using B, rep Row 1 and the Return Pass 1 twice.

Row 135: Using B, starting in the second st, TSS to last vertical bar, work end st.
Work Return Pass 3, changing to C.
Fasten off B.

Rows 136–171: Rep Rows 130–135 six more times.

Rows 172 and 173: Rep Rows 130 and 131 once more.

Row 174: Rep Row 130 once again.
On next Forward Pass row, bind (cast) off using C.

Making up and finishing

Weave in all ends and block to the desired measurements (see page 28).

TIP Tunisian crochet does tend to curl on the cast-on and bound- (cast-) off edges. You may find that blocking after every few wears will help to keep this neat shape.

Colorblock Bobble Hat

This chunky hat is worked flat using Tunisian Simple Stitch for a dense and cozy finish. Work this pattern in a pair of contrasting shades for a dramatic colorblock effect and finish with a fuzzy faux-fur pompom.

SKILL RATING: ●

YARN AND MATERIALS

Cascade 220 Superwash (100% wool) light worsted (DK) weight, approx 219yd (200m) per 3½oz (100g) ball
1 ball each of:
  Coral shade 827 (A)
  Aspen Heather shade 359 (B)

Faux fur pompom

HOOK AND EQUIPMENT

US size J-10 (6mm) Tunisian crochet hook

Yarn needle

FINISHED MEASUREMENTS

9½in (24cm) wide at brim when seamed and laid flat

8¾in (22.5cm) tall excluding pompom

GAUGE (TENSION)

8 sts x 8 rows = 2 x 2in (5 x 5cm) in Tunisian Simple Stitch using a US size J-10 (6mm) hook, after blocking.

ABBREVIATIONS

See page 31.

STITCHES USED

Tunisian Knit Stitch (TKS) (see page 15)

Tunisian Purl Stitch (TPS) (see page 16)

Tunisian Simple Stitch (TSS) (see page 14)

2TSStog: Decrease by working 2 stitches together using Tunisian Simple Stitch (see page 18)

NOTE

The last TPS stitch in the forward pass row will sit slightly differently on the hook so you will need to insert the hook carefully to avoid missing or twisting the stitch—see Techniques: End stitch (page 14)

Hat

Foundation chain and forward pass: Using A, ch80, starting in second ch from hook, working into back bumps of chain, pick up 79 sts for foundation row. (*80 loops on hook, 80 sts*)

Return pass 1: Yoh, draw through first st, *yoh, draw through next 2 sts on hook; rep from * to end. (*1 st on hook*)

Row 1: Starting in the second st, *TKS, TPS; rep from * to last vertical bar, work end st. (*80 sts*)
Work Return Pass 1.

Rows 2–5: Rep Row 1 and the Return Pass 1 four more times.

Row 6: Starting in the second st, TSS to last vertical bar, work end st. (*80 sts*)
Work Return Pass 1.
Rep Row 6 and the Return Pass 1 another 10 times.

Row 17: Starting in the second st, TSS to last vertical bar, work end st. (*80 sts*)

Return pass 2: Yoh, draw through first st, *yoh, draw through next 2 sts on hook; rep from * to last 2 sts on hook, join in B, yoh, draw through last 2 sts on hook. (*1 st on hook in B*)

Row 18: Starting in the second st, TSS to last vertical bar, work end st. (*80 sts*)
Work Return Pass 1.

Rows 19–24: Rep Row 18 and the Return Pass 1 six more times. (*1 st on hook*)

Row 25: Starting in the second st, TSS in next 2 sts, [2TSStog, TSS in next 6 sts] 9 times, 2TSStog, TSS in next 2 sts, work end st. (*70 sts*)
Work Return Pass 1. (*1 st on hook*)

Row 26: Starting in the second st, TSS in next 2 sts, [2TSStog, TSS in next 5 sts] 9 times, 2TSStog, TSS in next st, work end st. (*60 sts*)
Work Return Pass 1. (*1 st on hook*)

Row 27: Starting in the second st, TSS in next 2 sts, [2TSStog, TSS in next 4 sts] 9 times, 2TSStog, work end st. (*50 sts*)
Work Return Pass 1. (*1 st on hook*)

Row 28: Starting in the second st, TSS in next st, [2TSStog, TSS in next 3 sts] 9 times, 2TSStog, work end st. (*40 sts*)
Work Return Pass 1. (*1 st on hook*)

Row 29: Starting in the second st, [2TSStog, TSS in next 2 sts] 9 times, 2TSStog, work end st. (*30 sts*)
Work Return Pass 1. (*1 st on hook*)

Row 30: Starting in the second st, [2TSStog, TSS in next st] 9 times, TSS in next st, work end st. (*21 sts*)
Work Return Pass 1. (*1 st on hook*)

Row 31: Starting in the second st, [2TSStog] 9 times, TSS in next st, work end st. (*12 sts*)
On next Forward Pass row, bind (cast) off.

Make it yours

If you prefer to make a more slouchy version of this hat, simply work more rows before the increase to make it taller.

Making up and finishing

Weave in all ends and block to the desired measurements (see page 28). Once blocked, using a yarn needle and starting at the ribbing of the hat, work in mattress stitch (see page 29) to sew the center back seam. At the top of the hat take the yarn through stitches around the small opening and gather in, then sew in place to secure. Sew a faux fur pompom into place.

Triangle Shawl

This shawl is worked in lightweight lace yarn and uses increases both at the center and at each edge to grow into a wide triangle.

SKILL RATING: ● ●

YARN AND MATERIALS

Malabrigo Lace (100% merino wool) lace (2ply) weight yarn, approx 470yd (430m) per 1¾oz (50g) ball
   2 balls of Archangel shade 850

HOOKS AND EQUIPMENT

US size I-9 (5.5mm) Tunisian crochet hook with cable

US size L-11 (8mm) Tunisian crochet hook with cable

Yarn needle

Locking or split-ring stitch marker (optional)

FINISHED MEASUREMENTS

23½in (60cm) down center spine

63¾in (162cm) along neck edge

GAUGE (TENSION)

23 sts x 18 rows = 4 x 4in (10 x 10cm) in Tunisian Simple Stitch using a US size I-9 (5.5mm) hook, after blocking.

ABBREVIATIONS

See page 31.

STITCHES USED

Tunisian Knit Stitch (TKS) (see page 15)

Tunisian Simple Stitch (TSS) (see page 14)

Make 1 (M1TSS) (see page 20)

TIP This project works with increases at either side of the center stitch and at each end of the row, and, as the number of stitches builds rapidly, a Tunisian crochet hook with a cable is the best option to use.

Shawl

Foundation chain and forward pass: Using US size I-9 (5.5mm) ch5, starting in second ch from hook, working into back bumps of ch, pick up 4 sts for foundation row. (*5 loops on hook, 5 sts*)

Return pass: Yoh, draw through first st, *yoh, draw through next 2 sts on hook; rep from * to end. (*1 st on hook*)

Row 1: M1TSS, TSS, M1TSS, TKS (center st, PM if desired), M1TSS, TSS, M1TSS, work end st. (*9 sts*)
Work Return Pass.

Row 2: M1TSS, TSS in next 3 sts, M1TSS, TKS (center st), M1TSS, TSS in next 3 sts, M1TSS, work end st. (*13 sts*)
Work Return Pass.

Row 3: M1TSS, TSS in next 5 sts, M1TSS, TKS (center st), M1TSS, TSS in next 5 sts, M1TSS, work end st. (*17 sts*)
Work Return Pass.

Row 4: M1TSS, TSS in next 7 sts, M1TSS, TKS (center st), M1TSS, TSS in next 7 sts, M1TSS, work end st. (*21 sts*)
Work Return Pass.

Row 5: M1TSS, TSS in next 9 sts, M1TSS, TKS (center st), M1TSS, TSS in next 9 sts, M1TSS, work end st. (*25 sts*)
Work Return Pass.

Row 6: M1TSS, TSS in next 11 sts, M1TSS, TKS (center st), M1TSS, TSS in next 11 sts, M1TSS, work end st. (*29 sts*)
Work Return Pass.

Row 7: M1TSS, TSS in next 13 sts, M1TSS, TKS (center st), M1TSS, TSS in next 13 sts, M1TSS, work end st. (*33 sts*)
Work Return Pass.

Row 8: M1TSS, TSS in next 15 sts, M1TSS, TKS (center st), M1TSS, TSS in next 15 sts, M1TSS, work end st. (*37 sts*)
Work Return Pass.

Row 9: M1TSS, TSS in next 17 sts, M1TSS, TKS (center st), M1TSS, TSS in next 17 sts, M1TSS, work end st. (*41 sts*)
Work Return Pass.

Row 10: M1TSS, TSS in next 19 sts, M1TSS, TKS (center st), M1TSS, TSS in next 19 sts, M1TSS, work end st. (*45 sts*)
Work Return Pass.

Cont working in pattern as set, increasing by 4 sts with each Forward Pass row until you have worked Row 81. (*329 sts*)
Change to US size L-11 (8mm) hook.
Cont as set for a further 6 rows. (*353 sts*)
On next Forward Pass row, bind (cast) off.

Making up and finishing

Weave in all ends and block flat to the desired measurements (see page 28).

Chevron Scarf

Create dramatic chevron shaping by working with a pattern of increases and decreases across the row. Team two bold shades with a neutral for a real stand-out scarf.

SKILL RATING: ●

YARN AND MATERIALS

West Yorkshire Spinners ColourLab (100% wool) light worsted (DK) weight, approx 246yd (225m) per 3½oz (100g) ball
1 ball each of:
 Coral Crush shade 361 (A)
 Arctic White shade 011 (B)
 Sky Blue shade 1136 (C)

HOOK AND EQUIPMENT

US size K-10½ (6.5mm) Tunisian crochet hook

Yarn needle

FINISHED MEASUREMENTS

86 x 5in (218 x 13cm)

GAUGE (TENSION)

16.5 sts x 16.5 rows = 4 x 4in (10 x 10cm) in Tunisian Simple Stitch worked straight using a US size K-10½ (6.5mm) hook.

ABBREVIATIONS

See page 31.

STITCHES USED

Tunisian Simple Stitch (TSS) (see page 14)

Make 1 (M1) (see page 20)

Tunisian Simple Stitch 3 together (TSS3tog) (see page 19)

Scarf

Foundation chain and forward pass: Using A, ch29, starting in second ch from hook, working into back bumps of chain, pick up 28 sts for foundation row. (*29 loops on hook, 29 sts*)

Return pass: Yoh, draw through first st, *yoh, draw through next 2 sts on hook; rep from * to end. (*1 st on hook*)

Row 1: Starting in second st, M1, TSS in next 5 sts, TSS3tog, TSS in next 5 sts, M1, TSS, M1, TSS in next 5 sts, TSS3tog, TSS in next 5 sts, M1, work end st.
Work Return Pass.
Rep Row 1 and Return Pass, working foll color sequence.
Cont in yarn A for 10 more rows.
Using B: 2 rows.
Using C: 11 rows.
Using B: 22 rows.
*Using A: 11 rows.
Using B: 2 rows.
Using C: 11 rows.
Using B: 22 rows.
Rep color sequence from * three more times.
Using A: 11 rows.
Using B: 2 rows.
Using C: 11 rows.
On next Forward Pass row, bind (cast) off in TSS using C.

Making up and finishing

Weave in all ends and block flat to the desired measurements (see page 28).

. . . .

Make it yours

This chevron design is created using a pattern of increases and decreases. If you want to make a wider scarf or create a wrap, you can increase the width to your chosen size by casting on stitches to a multiple of 14 + 1.

. . . .

Cozy Cowl

A warm cowl looped around your neck is a stylish way to beat the winter chills. This design is worked in a bright hot pink for maximum impact, and the bulky yarn makes this a satisfyingly quick project.

SKILL RATING: ●

YARN AND MATERIALS

Debbie Bliss Super Chunky Merino (100% merino wool) bulky (chunky) weight, approx 87yd (80m) per 3½oz (100g) ball
   2 balls of Hot Pink shade 13

HOOK AND EQUIPMENT

US size P-16/Q (12mm) Tunisian crochet hook

Yarn needle

FINISHED MEASUREMENTS

16 x 8¼in (41 x 21cm) when folded

GAUGE (TENSION)

8.5 sts x 7 rows = 4 x 4in (10 x 10cm) in Tunisian Simple Stitch using a US size P-16/Q (12mm) hook.

ABBREVIATIONS

See page 31.

STITCH USED

Tunisian Simple Stitch (TSS) (see page 14)

Cowl

Foundation chain and forward pass: Ch18, starting in second ch from hook, working into back bumps of chain, pick up 17 sts for foundation row. (*18 loops on hook, 18 sts*)

Return pass: Yoh, draw through first st, *yoh, draw through next 2 sts on hook; rep from * to end. (*1 st on hook*)

Row 1: Starting in second st, TSS to last vertical bar, work end st. (*18 sts*)

Work Return Pass.

Rep Row 1 and Return Pass, maintaining st count on Forward Pass until work measures 33½in (85cm) long. On next Forward Pass row, bind (cast) off.

Making up and finishing

Weave in all ends and block flat to the desired measurements (see page 28).

Align the two shorter edges and thread a yarn needle with a yarn tail. Sew together using mattress stitch (see page 29).

Fasten off and weave in ends.

Make it yours

This cowl is simply a crochet strip joined at the ends to make a loop—it is an ideal project to customize. You could make it wider by adding more stitches to the foundation, or longer by working more rows. Alternatively, it's a perfect blank canvas for adding stripes or a colorblock design with your favorite shades.

Textured Wrap

Tunisian Smock Stitch creates a repeated woven pattern and here it is worked in a smooth cotton yarn to give this wrap a deluxe finish.

SKILL RATING: ● ●

YARN AND MATERIALS

MillaMia Naturally Soft Cotton (100% cotton) sport (4ply) weight yarn, approx 180yd (165m) per 1¾oz (50g) ball
    4 balls of Indigo Purple shade 321

HOOK AND EQUIPMENT

US size K-10½ (6.5mm) Tunisian crochet hook

Yarn needle

FINISHED MEASUREMENTS

5 x 58¼in (13 x 148cm)

GAUGE (TENSION)

18 sts x 15 rows = 4 x 4in (10 x 10cm) in Tunisian Smock Stitch using a US size K-10½ (6mm) hook, after blocking.

ABBREVIATIONS

See page 31.

STITCHES USED

Tunisian Smock Stitch made of alt YU and 2TSStog (see page 22)

Tunisian Simple Stitch (TSS) (see page 14)

Tunisian Simple Stitch 2 together (2TSStog) (see page 18)

Wrap

Foundation chain and forward pass: Ch60, starting in second ch from hook, working into back bumps of chain, pick up 59 sts for foundation row. *(60 loops on hook, 60 sts)*

Return pass: Yoh, draw through first st, *yoh, draw through next 2 sts on hook; rep from * to end. *(1 st on hook)*

BORDER

Row 1: Starting in second st, TSS in each st to last vertical bar, work end st.
Work Return Pass.

MAIN SECTION

Row 2: TSS in second st from hook, *2TSStog, YU; rep from * to last 2 sts, TSS in next st, work end st.
Work Return Pass.

Row 3: Starting in second st from hook, TSS in next 2 sts, *2TSStog, YU; rep from * to last 3 sts, TSS in next 2 sts, work end st.
Work Return Pass.
Smock st is a two-row repeat, rep Rows 2 and 3 until work measures 58in (147cm).

BORDER

Next row: Starting in second st, TSS in each st to last vertical bar, work end st.
Work Return Pass.
Bind (cast) off.

Making up and finishing

Weave in all ends and block flat to the desired measurements (see page 28).

TIPS Tunisian Smock Stitch is a two-stitch pattern repeated over two rows. The smock stitch design is created by alternating yarn under—as opposed to a yarn over—and Tunisian Simple Stitch 2 Together across the row. Be sure to create this section of the stitch in the correct orientation to ensure the smock stitch is made.

To ensure the edges of the wrap are neat there is a border on each side; the first and last stitches (before end stitch) are worked in Tunisian Simple Stitch.

Simple Two-seam Bolero

Worked in a lightweight yarn and using large drop stitches, this floaty bolero is a pretty cover-up for summer evenings. The garment can be custom-sized to suit your own measurements, too!

SKILL RATING: ●●

YARN AND MATERIALS

Berroco Dulce (50% cotton, 20% nylon, 16% alpaca, 14% wool) worsted (Aran) weight yarn, approx 175yd (160m) per 1¾oz (50g) ball
  2 balls of Turquoise shade 2035

Alternative yarn
Berroco Mistico (48% cotton, 30% alpaca, 12% wool, 10% nylon,) worsted (Aran) weight yarn, approx 191yd (175m) per 1¾oz (50g) ball
  2 balls of Pensive shade 2522

HOOK AND EQUIPMENT

US size L-11 (8mm) Tunisian crochet hook

Yarn needle

FINISHED MEASUREMENTS

32¼ x 20½in (82 x 52cm) when laid flat

GAUGE (TENSION)

11.5 sts x 11 rows = 4 x 4in (10 x 10cm) in Tunisian Simple Stitch using an US size L-11 (8mm) hook, after blocking.

ABBREVIATIONS

See page 31.

STITCHES USED

Drop Stitch (drop st) (see page 24)

Yarn Over (YO) (see page 23)

Tunisian Simple Stitch (TSS) (see page 14)

Bolero

Foundation chain and forward pass: Ch60, starting in second ch from hook, working into back bumps of chain, pick up 59 sts for foundation row. (*60 loops on hook, 60 sts*)

Return pass: Yoh, draw through first st, *yoh, draw through next 2 sts on hook; rep from * to end. (*1 st on hook*)

Row 1: Starting in second st, *TSS in each st to last vertical bar, work end st. (*60 sts*)
Work Return Pass.

Rows 2–6: Rep Row 1 and Return Pass 5 more times.

Row 7: Ch1 (turning ch as sts will be taller), *YO, TSS rep from * to last st, YO, work end st.

Return pass for drop st rows: Ch1 (turning ch as sts will be taller), yoh, draw through first st, *yoh, draw through next 2 sts on hook, drop YO to create drop st; rep from * to end. (*1 st on hook*)

Rows 8–12: Rep Row 7 and Return Pass for Drop St rows 5 more times.

Rows 13–15: Rep Row 1 and Return Pass 3 times.
Rep Rows 7–15 three more times.

Rows 42–44: Rep Row 1 and Return Pass 3 times.
Bind (cast) off.

Making up and finishing

Weave in all ends and block flat to the desired measurements (see page 28).

Fold the strip in half, aligning the long edges, and thread a yarn needle with the yarn tail. Work in mattress stitch (see page 29) to secure the side seam along the end sections of six rows of Tunisian Simple Stitch to form a cuff at each end. Fasten off and weave in all yarn ends.

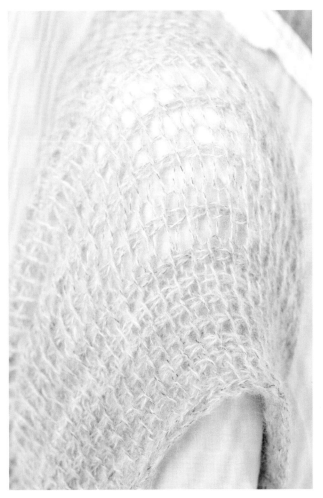

TIPS This garment can be changed in size due to its simple construction. The bolero is created from a rectangle that is folded then seamed under the arms on each side. Custom-size your bolero by measuring from your neck to your waist to give the width of the rectangle, and from mid-forearm to mid-forearm with your arms outstretched for the length.

Drop stitches and a sized-up hook are used here to create the open fabric of these lacy style stitches. Be sure not to work the yarn you've taken over the hook on the Return Pass, instead allowing each one to drop from the hook and extend the length of the stitches worked.

Chapter 2

Decorations & Home Accessories

Placemat

Handcrafted placemats add a special touch to your table settings. This two-color design creates a woven effect with alternating yarns.

SKILL RATING: ●

YARN AND MATERIALS

Schachenmayr Catania (100% cotton) sport (4ply) weight, approx 137yd (125m) per 1¾oz (50g) ball
1 ball each of:
   Graublau shade 269 (blue) (A)
   Bast shade 257 (beige) (B)

HOOK AND EQUIPMENT

US size H-8 (5mm) Tunisian crochet hook

Yarn needle

FINISHED MEASUREMENTS

14¼ x 9¾in (36 x 25cm)

GAUGE (TENSION)

17 sts x 15 rows = 4 x 4in (10 x 10cm) in Tunisian Simple Stitch using a US size H-8 (5mm) hook.

ABBREVIATIONS

See page 31.

STITCH USED

Tunisian Simple Stitch (TSS) (see page 14)

Placemat

Foundation chain and forward pass: Using A, ch45, starting in second ch from hook, working into back bumps of chain, pick up 44 sts for foundation row. (*45 loops on hook, 45 sts*)
Return pass: Yoh, draw through first st, *yoh, draw through next 2 sts on hook; rep from * to end. (*1 st on hook*)
Row 1: Starting in second st, TSS to last vertical bar, work end st. (*45 sts*)
Work Return Pass.
Row 2: Starting in second st, TSS to last vertical bar, work end st. (*45 sts*)
Work Return Pass changing to B on the first yoh, draw through first st.
Row 3: Using B, starting in second st, TSS to last vertical bar, work end st. (*45 sts*)
Work Return Pass changing to A on the first yoh, draw through first st.
Rep Row 2 and Return Pass, maintaining st count on Forward Pass, alternating yarn colors at the beginning of each return pass until work measures 13½in (34cm) long.
Cont in A, rep Row 1 and Return Pass.
On next Forward Pass row, bind (cast) off.

Making up and finishing

Weave in all ends and block flat to the desired measurements (see page 28).

TIP The woven effect of the two colors of yarn is created by alternating between the two shades at the beginning of the return pass. This also means that, because the yarns are changed at the same side each time, you can carry the unused yarn along the side of the work, so you have fewer yarn tails to weave in at the end of the project.

Pot Holders

Embrace cottage-core with some handmade pot holders.
You can also pass your favorite dishes around the table
with these rustic mitts.

SKILL RATING: ●

YARN AND MATERIALS

Rico Creative Cotton Aran (100%
cotton) worsted (Aran) weight, approx
93yd (85m) per 1¾oz (50g) ball
1 ball each of:
   Clay shade 51 (light peach)
   Smoky Berry shade 12 (pink)

HOOK AND EQUIPMENT

US size K-10½ (6.5mm) Tunisian
crochet hook

Yarn needle

FINISHED MEASUREMENTS

Main section: 7in (18cm) square

Pocket: 7 x 3¼in (18 x 8cm)

GAUGE (TENSION)

13.5 sts x 13 rows = 4 x 4in (10 x
10cm) in Tunisian Simple Stitch
using a US size K-10½ (6.5mm) hook.

ABBREVIATIONS

See page 31.

STITCH USED

Tunisian Simple Stitch (TSS)
(see page 14)

Main section

(make one in each color)

Foundation chain and forward pass: Ch20, starting in second ch from hook, working into back bumps of chain, pick up 19 sts for foundation row. (*20 loops on hook, 20 sts*)

Return pass: Yoh, draw through first st, *yoh, draw through next 2 sts on hook; rep from * to end. (*1 st on hook*)

Row 1: Starting in second st, TSS to last vertical bar, work end st. (*20 sts*)

Work Return Pass.

Rep Row 1 and Return Pass 19 more times. (*20 rows*)

On next Forward Pass row, bind (cast) off.

Pocket

(make one in each color)

Foundation chain and forward pass: Ch20, starting in second ch from hook, working into back bumps of chain, pick up 19 sts for foundation row. (*20 loops on hook, 20 sts*)

Return pass: Yoh, draw through first st, *yoh, draw through next 2 sts on hook; rep from * to end. (*1 st on hook*)

Row 1: Starting in second st, TSS to last vertical bar, work end st. (*20 sts*)

Work Return Pass.

Rep Row 1 and the Return Pass 9 more times. (*10 rows*)

On next Forward Pass row, bind (cast) off.

Making up and finishing

Weave in all ends and block flat to the desired measurements (see page 28).

Working with each pot holder and pocket in turn, place the pocket onto the main section with the RS of both uppermost and ensuring the correct orientation of the stitches. Using the hook and matching yarn, join work around the entire outer edge with 1sl st in each stitch, making sure to work through the pocket and the main to join the pocket on three sides.

Fasten off and weave in ends.

TIP These pot holders feature small pockets for your hands, meaning that once your fingers are inside they won't slip while you are moving warmed dishes. Note: due to the materials used these are not recommended for use for items direct from the oven.

Storage Basket

Created from a round crochet base, this handy storage tub—worked in sturdy macramé cord—is a versatile caddy for stowing household items.

SKILL RATING: ● ●

YARN AND MATERIALS

Macramé cord (100% cotton) bulky (chunky) weight, approx 88yd (81m) per 7oz (200g) ball

1 ball each of:
  Ecru (A)
  Green (B)

2¼ x 4in (6 x 10cm) piece of cork fabric

2 ball head stud rivets with screw back, ⁵/₁₆in (8mm) size

HOOK AND EQUIPMENT

US size P-16/Q (12mm) Tunisian crochet hook

Yarn needle

Locking or split-ring stitch marker

Hole punch

FINISHED MEASUREMENTS

5½in (14cm) base diameter

5in (13cm) high

GAUGE (TENSION)

8.5 sts x 6.5 rows = 4 x 4in (10 x 10cm) in Tunisian Simple Stitch using a US size P-16/Q (12mm) hook.

ABBREVIATIONS

See page 31.

STITCHES USED

Tunisian Simple Stitch (TSS) (see page 14)

Magic ring (see page 26)

Single crochet (sc) (see page 27)

NOTE

This pattern works with standard crochet and Tunisian Crochet.

Make it yours

You can change the size of the basket by working a larger base to make it wider, or working longer or shorter Tunisian crochet rows to adjust the height.

Base

Using B, make a magic ring.
Round 1: 6sc into ring. (*6 sts*)
PM at start of round.
Round 2: [2sc in next st] 6 times. (*12 sts*)
Round 3: [1sc in next st, 2sc in next st] 6 times. (*18 sts*)
Round 4: [1sc in next 2 sts, 2sc in next st] 6 times. (*24 sts*)
Round 5: [1sc in next 3 sts, 2sc in next st] 6 times. (*30 sts*)
Round 6: [1sc in next 4 sts, 2sc in next st] 6 times. (*36 sts*)
Fasten off B.

Sides

Begin working in Tunisian Simple Stitch.
Foundation chain and forward pass: Using B, ch8, starting in second ch from hook, working into back bumps of chain, pick up 7 sts for foundation row. (*8 loops on hook, 8 sts*)
Return pass: Pass hook through BLO of next st in crochet circle base, yoh and draw through first st, *yoh, draw through next 2 sts on hook; rep from * to end.
Row 1: Starting in second st, TSS to last vertical bar, work end st. (*8 sts*)
Work Return Pass.
Rep Row 1 and Return Pass 33 more times, ending on a Return Pass.
Fasten off B, join in A.
Round 1: 1sc in each row end around the top of the basket. (*36 sts*)
Round 2: 1sc in each st.
Fasten off.

TIPS If you are using a long Tunisian Crochet hook for your project, you may also need a US size P-16/Q (12mm) standard hook for the single crochet base section, so that the extra length doesn't make it awkward to work the stitches. Alternatively, a Tunisian hook with a cable is pretty versatile and can be used for smaller and larger elements alike.

Macramé cord has a stiffer finish than bulky yarns, which will give the storage basket a more robust finish. I used Knitcraft Return of the Mac Yarn for this project.

Making up and finishing

Align the two straight edges and thread a yarn needle with the yarn tail. Work in mattress stitch (see page 29) to secure the side seam from the top of the basket to the foundation circle.
Fasten off.
Weave in all yarn ends (see page 28).
Add an accent by folding a 2¼ x 4in (6 x 10cm) piece of cork fabric so that the long raw edges are aligned into the center (as with making bias tape). Fold in half and place over the upper edge of the basket. Punch two holes and insert two ball rivets evenly spaced into the back layer of the cork fabric and through the crochet, then punch two holes into the front layer to correspond with the rivets and screw on the backs to secure.

Dishcloth

Keep your dishes sparkling with a handmade dishcloth. This small project features a distinctive honeycomb stitch and makes a great housewarming gift.

SKILL RATING: ●

YARN AND MATERIALS

Lion Brand 24/7 Cotton (100% cotton) worsted (Aran) weight, approx 186yd (170m) per 3½oz (100g) ball
  1 ball of Creamsicle shade 132

HOOK AND EQUIPMENT

US size K-10½ (6.5mm) Tunisian crochet hook

Yarn needle

FINISHED MEASUREMENTS

6¼in (16cm) square

GAUGE (TENSION)

11 sts x 12 rows = 4 x 4in (10 x 10cm) in Honeycomb Stitch using a US size K-10½ (6.5mm) hook with yarn held double.

ABBREVIATIONS

See page 31.

STITCHES USED

Honeycomb Stitch made of:

Tunisian Simple Stitch (TSS) (see page 14)

Tunisian Purl Stitch (TPS) (see page 16)

Dishcloth

Foundation chain and forward pass: With yarn held double throughout, ch19, starting in second ch from hook, working into back bumps of chain, pick up 18 sts for foundation row. (*19 loops on hook, 19 sts*)
Return pass: Yoh, draw through first st, *yoh, draw through next 2 sts on hook; rep from * to end. (*1 st on hook*)
Row 1: Starting in second st, 1TSS, *1TPS, 1TSS; rep from * to last vertical bar, work end st. (*19 sts*) Work Return Pass.
Row 2: Starting in second st, 1TPS, *1TSS , 1TPS; rep from * to last vertical bar, work end st. (*19 sts*) Work Return Pass.
Rep Row 1 and Return Pass, then Row 2 and Return Pass, another 8 times.
On next Forward Pass row, bind (cast) off in TSS, don't cut yarn.
Ch12, sl st in same sp to make hanging loop at corner. Fasten off.

Making up and finishing

Weave in all ends and block flat to the desired measurements (see page 28).

TIPS Honeycomb Stitch has a lovely texture and is created with a two-row pattern repeat. The Tunisian Simple Stitches and Tunisian Purl Stitches are alternated on the first row. On the second row these are alternated in the reversed order—so you will work simple stitch into the purl stitch from previous row and vice versa.

To get a really dense fabric for the dishcloth the yarn is held double throughout.

Circle Coasters

These pretty coasters are created from a foundation of standard crochet stitches worked in the round before transitioning to Tunisian crochet and working with short rows to create the circle shaping.

SKILL RATING: ●

YARN AND MATERIALS

Rico Baby Cotton Soft Print DK (50% acrylic, 50% cotton) light worsted (DK) weight, approx 137yd (125m) per 1¾oz (50g) ball
   1 ball of Azalea-Yellow shade 032

HOOK AND EQUIPMENT

US size H-8 (5mm) Tunisian crochet hook

Yarn needle

Locking or split-ring stitch marker

FINISHED MEASUREMENTS

4in (10cm) diameter

GAUGE (TENSION)

16 sts x 17 rows = 4 x 4in (10 x 10cm) in Tunisian Simple Stitch using a US size H-8 (5mm) hook.

ABBREVIATIONS

See page 31.

STITCHES USED

Magic ring (see page 26)

Single crochet (sc) (see page 27)

Tunisian Simple Stitch (TSS) (see page 14)

Coaster

(make 2)

Make a magic ring.

Round 1: 6sc into ring. (*6 sts*)

PM at start of round.

Round 2: [2sc in next st] 6 times. (*12 sts*)

Begin working in TSS with short row shaping.

Foundation chain and forward pass: Sl st into first st in foundation circle, ch6, starting in second ch from hook, working into back bumps of chain, pick up 5 sts for foundation row. (*6 loops on hook, 6 sts*)

Return pass 1: Sl st in next st in foundation circle, *yoh, draw through next 2 sts on hook; rep from * to end. (*1 st on hook*)

Row 1: Starting in second st, TSS in next 3 sts. (*4 loops on hook, 4 sts*)

Return pass 2: Sl st in next TSS st, *yoh, draw through next 2 sts on hook; rep from * to end. (*1 st on hook*)

Row 2: TSS in the next 4 sts. (*5 loops on hook, 5 sts*)

Work Return Pass 2.

Row 3: TSS in next 5 sts. (*6 loops on hook, 6 sts*)

Work Return Pass 1.

Row 4: TSS in next 3 sts. (*4 loops on hook, 4 sts*)

Work Return Pass 2.

Row 5: TSS in next 3 sts of last row, then TSS in 1 st of row below last row. (*5 loops on hook, 5 sts*)

Work Return Pass 2.

Row 6: TSS in next 4 sts of last row, then TSS in 1 st of row below last row. (*6 loops on hoop, 6 sts*)

Work Return Pass 1.

Rep Rows 4–6 and Return Pass as set 12 more times, ending after a Return Pass with 1 loop on hook.

Join with a sl st and work around outer edge of circle with 1sc in each st.

Fasten off.

Making up and finishing

Block flat as desired (see page 28).

Align the two edges and thread a yarn needle with the yarn tail. Work in mattress stitch (see page 29) to secure the side seam from the edge of the circle to the foundation circle.

Fasten off.

Weave in all yarn ends (see page 28).

TIPS If you are using a long Tunisian Crochet hook for your project you may also need a US size H-8 (5mm) standard hook for the single crochet base section, so that the extra length doesn't make it awkward to work the stitches. Alternatively, a Tunisian hook with a cable is very versatile and can be used for smaller and larger elements alike.

The initial foundation of the coasters is worked in crochet in the round in a continuous spiral with no chain stitch between one round and the next. Place a locking or split-ring stitch marker on the first stitch of the round to help keep track of the round.

The coaster is created in rows of Tunisian Simple Stitch worked in toward the foundation circle. To achieve the full, flat circle short rows are introduced. This shaping technique means only working a portion of the stitches on a set row to provide width to a specific area—here the outer edge of the circle. When working a row after the short row, slip stitch into the stitch below the last stitch of the short row—this will help to prevent gaps in the fabric around the shaping.

Wall Hanging

Add a pop of color to your rooms with a cheerful rainbow wall hanging. This design is worked in Tunisian Simple Stitch, making it the ideal canvas for a graphic motif.

SKILL RATING: ● ●

YARN AND MATERIALS

Caron Simply Soft (100% acrylic) worsted (Aran) weight yarn, approx 315yd (288m) per 6oz (170g) ball

    1 ball each of:
    Off White shade 9702 (A)
    Persimmon shade 9754 (dark orange) (B)
    Robin's Egg shade 9780 (turquoise) (C)
    Country Blue shade 9710 (D)

11½in (29cm) of dowling

Twine

HOOKS AND EQUIPMENT

US size K-10½ (6.5mm) Tunisian crochet hook

US size N-15 (10mm) Tunisian crochet hook

Yarn needle

FINISHED MEASUREMENTS

8 x 9in (20.5 x 23cm) excluding tassels and hanging loops

GAUGE (TENSION)

14 sts x 12 rows = 4 x 4in (10 x 10cm) in Tunisian Simple Stitch using a US size K-10½ (6.5mm) hook, after blocking.

ABBREVIATIONS

See page 31.

STITCH USED

Tunisian Simple Stitch (TSS) (see page 14)

Make it yours

As this project needs lots of color changes across the rows, you may prefer to ball up a few small balls of each color to allow you to work on each color as it is needed in the pattern. Using separate balls of color means that there is no need to carry the yarn across the back of the work, which helps maintain a consistent gauge (tension).

Wall hanging

Foundation chain and forward pass: Using A, ch30, starting in second ch from hook, working into back bumps of chain, pick up 29 sts for foundation row. (*30 loops on hook, 30 sts*)

Return pass: Yoh, draw through first st, *yoh, draw through next 2 sts on hook; rep from * to end. (*1 st on hook*)

Row 1: Starting in second st, TSS in next 6 sts using A, TSS in next 2 sts using D, TSS in next 2 sts using C, TSS in next 2 sts using B, TSS in next 4 sts using A, TSS in next 2 sts using B, TSS in next 2 sts using C, TSS in next 2 sts using D, TSS in next 6 sts using A, work end st.
Work Return Pass changing color to correspond with color used on Forward Pass.

Rows 2–8: Rep Row 1 and the Return Pass.

Row 9: Starting in second st, TSS in next 6 sts using A, TSS in next 2 sts using D, TSS in next 2 sts using C, TSS in next 3 sts using B, TSS in next 2 sts using A, TSS in next 3 sts using B, TSS in next 2 sts using C, TSS in next 2 sts using D, TSS in next 6 sts using A, work end st.
Work Return Pass changing color to correspond with color used on Forward Pass.

Row 10: Starting in second st, TSS in next 6 sts using A, TSS in next 2 sts using D, TSS in next 3 sts using C, TSS in next 6 sts using B, TSS in next 3 sts using C, TSS in next 2 sts using D, TSS in next 6 sts using A, work end st.
Work Return Pass changing color to correspond with color used on Forward Pass.

Row 11: Starting in second st, TSS in next 7 sts using A, TSS in next 2 sts using D, TSS in next 3 sts using C, TSS in next 4 sts using B, TSS in next 3 sts using C, TSS in next 2 sts using D, TSS in next 7 sts using A, work end st.
Work Return Pass changing color to correspond with color used on Forward Pass.

Row 12: Starting in second st, TSS in next 7 sts using A, TSS in next 3 sts using D, TSS in next 8 sts using C, TSS in next 3 sts using D, TSS in next 7 sts using A, work end st.
Work Return Pass changing color to correspond with color used on Forward Pass.

Row 13: Starting in second st, TSS in next 8 sts using A, TSS in next 3 sts using D, TSS in next 6 sts using C, TSS in next 3 sts using D, TSS in next 8 sts using A, work end st.
Work Return Pass changing color to correspond with color used on Forward Pass.

Row 14: Starting in second st, TSS in next 9 sts using A, TSS in next 10 sts using D, TSS in next 9 sts using A, work end st.
Work Return Pass changing color to correspond with color used on Forward Pass.
Row 15: Starting in second st, TSS in next 11 sts using A, TSS in next 6 sts using D, TSS in next 11 sts using A, work end st.
Work Return Pass changing color to correspond with color used on Forward Pass.
Rows 16–25: Cont in A, starting in second st, TSS in each st to last vertical bar, work end st.
Work Return Pass.
Row 26: Change to US size N-15 (10mm) hook, starting in second st, TSS in each st to last vertical bar, work end st.
Fasten off.

Making up and finishing

Weave in all ends and block flat to the desired measurements (see page 28).
Thread the dowling through the large looped stitches at the top. Secure a length of twine to either end of the dowel to make a hanging loop.
Cut twelve 12in (30cm) strands each of B, C, and D. Working with three strands in turn, fold in half and create a lark's head knot tassel to correspond with each colored section along the lower edge (see page 30). Trim the tassels to neaten.

Hanging Basket

This hanging basket is great for adding a unique accent to your interiors—use it for displaying precious houseplants or tidying away small items.

SKILL RATING: ● ●

YARN AND MATERIALS

Wool And The Gang Jersey Be Good (98% cotton, 2% elastane) upcycled T-shirt yarn, super bulky (super chunky) weight, approx 109yd (100m) per 18oz (500g) ball
 1 ball of Cuppa T

2¾in (7cm) diameter wooden ring

HOOK AND EQUIPMENT

US size P-16/Q (12mm) Tunisian crochet hook

Yarn needle

FINISHED MEASUREMENTS

13¾in (35cm) tall x 8½in (21.5cm) wide (at seamed base)

GAUGE (TENSION)

6 sts x 5 rows = 4 x 4in (10 x 10cm) in Tunisian Simple Stitch using a US size P-16/Q (12mm) hook.

ABBREVIATIONS

See page 31.

STITCHES USED

Tunisian Simple Stitch 2 together (2TSStog) (see page 18)

Tunisian Simple Stitch (see page 14)

Make it yours

The hanging basket is created by folding a triangular piece of Tunisian simple stitch, the shaping worked by decreasing at the start and ends of the row. You can make your own custom-size basket by making a larger or smaller triangle.

Basket

Foundation chain and forward pass: Ch35, starting in second ch from hook, working into back bumps of chain, pick up 34 sts for foundation row. (*35 loops on hook, 35 sts*)

Return pass: Yoh, draw through first st, *yoh, draw through next 2 sts on hook; rep from * to end. (*1 st on hook*)

Row 1: Starting in second st, 2TSStog, TSS in each st to last 3 sts, 2TSStog, work end st. (*33 sts*)
Work Return Pass.

Row 2: Starting in second st, 2TSStog, TSS in each st to last 3 sts, 2TSStog, work end st. (*31 sts*)
Work Return Pass.

Row 3: Starting in second st, 2TSStog, TSS in each st to last 3 sts, 2TSStog, work end st. (*29 sts*)
Work Return Pass.

Cont in pattern as set, dec at start and end of each Forward Pass and working Return Pass until 3 sts remain.

Row 15: Starting in second st, TSS in vertical bar, work end st. (*3 sts*)
Work Return Pass.

Rep Row 15 and Return Pass twice more.

On next Forward Pass row, bind (cast) off in TSS, don't cut yarn.

TIP Ensure that the wooden ring is stitched firmly in place before filling the basket—especially if you are using it with delicate plants or in a child's room.

Making up and finishing

Block flat as desired (see page 28).

With WS uppermost, fold in the lower corners to create a pocket measuring 8½in (21.5cm) along the base. Thread a yarn needle with the yarn tail. Work in running stitch to secure the lower seam from edge to edge (see page 30). Fasten off.

Fold over the strip at the top and feed through the center of a wooden ring. Thread the yarn tail onto a yarn needle and use running stitch to secure the hanging loop at the top of the basket.

Weave in all yarn ends (see page 28).

Butterfly Mobile

Add a pretty accent to a nursery or child's room with this sweet crochet butterfly mobile. This project uses a very small amount of yarn, so you can choose some favorite colors from your stash!

SKILL RATING: ● ●

YARN AND MATERIALS

Sirdar Happy Cotton (100% cotton) light worsted (DK) weight yarn, approx 47yd (43m) per ¾oz (20g) ball

  1 ball each of:
  Bubblegum shade 799 (bright pink)
  Melon shade 794 (mustard yellow)
  Sorbet shade 793 (peach)
  Bubbly shade 785 (light blue)
  Bunting shade 797 (dark blue)
  Currant Bun shade 756 (purple)

Small amount of gray light worsted (DK) yarn for accents

6in (15cm) diameter metal ring

Ribbon or tape to cover ring (optional)

Fabric glue

Thread for stringing elements

Wooden beads to decorate (optional)

Ribbon for hanging loop

HOOK AND EQUIPMENT

US size I-9 (5.5mm) Tunisian crochet hook

Yarn needle

FINISHED MEASUREMENTS

2¾ x 2¾in (7 x 7cm) max width and length per butterfly

GAUGE (TENSION)

Exact gauge is not important in this project.

ABBREVIATIONS

See page 31.

STITCHES USED

Tunisian Simple Stitch 2 together (2TSStog) (see page 18)

Tunisian Simple Stitch (TSS) (see page 14)

Magic ring (see page 26)

Make 1 (M1TSS) (see page 20)

Butterfly

(make 1 in each color)

LARGE WING 1

Make a magic ring.

Foundation chain and forward pass: Ch8, starting in second ch from hook, working into back bumps of chain, pick up 7 sts for foundation row. (*8 loops on hook, 8 sts*) Sl st into magic ring.

Return pass: Yoh, draw through first st, *yoh, draw through next 2 sts on hook; rep from * to end. (*1 st on hook*)

Row 1: Starting in second st, 2TSStog, TSS to end, sl st into magic ring. (*7 sts*)
Work Return Pass.

Row 2: Starting in second st, 2TSStog, TSS to end, sl st into magic ring. (*6 sts*)
Work Return Pass.

Row 3: Starting in second st, 2TSStog, TSS to end, sl st into magic ring. (*5 sts*)
Work Return Pass.

Row 4: Starting in second st, 2TSStog, TSS to end, sl st into magic ring. (*4 sts*)
Work Return Pass.

Row 5: Starting in second st, 2TSStog, TSS to end, sl st into magic ring. (*3 sts*)
Work Return Pass.
Bind (cast) off, don't cut yarn.

SMALL WING 1

Foundation chain and forward pass: Ch5, starting in second ch from hook, working into back bumps of chain, pick up 4 sts for foundation row. (*5 loops on hook, 5 sts*) Sl st into magic ring, continuing counterclockwise around the ring from the last sl st.

Return pass: Yoh, draw through first st, *yoh, draw through next 2 sts on hook; rep from * to end. (*1 st on hook*)

Row 1: Starting in second st, 2TSStog, TSS to end, sl st into magic ring. (*4 sts*)
Work Return Pass.

Row 2: Starting in second st, 2TSStog, TSS to end, sl st into magic ring. (*3 sts*)
Work Return Pass.
Bind (cast) off, don't cut yarn.

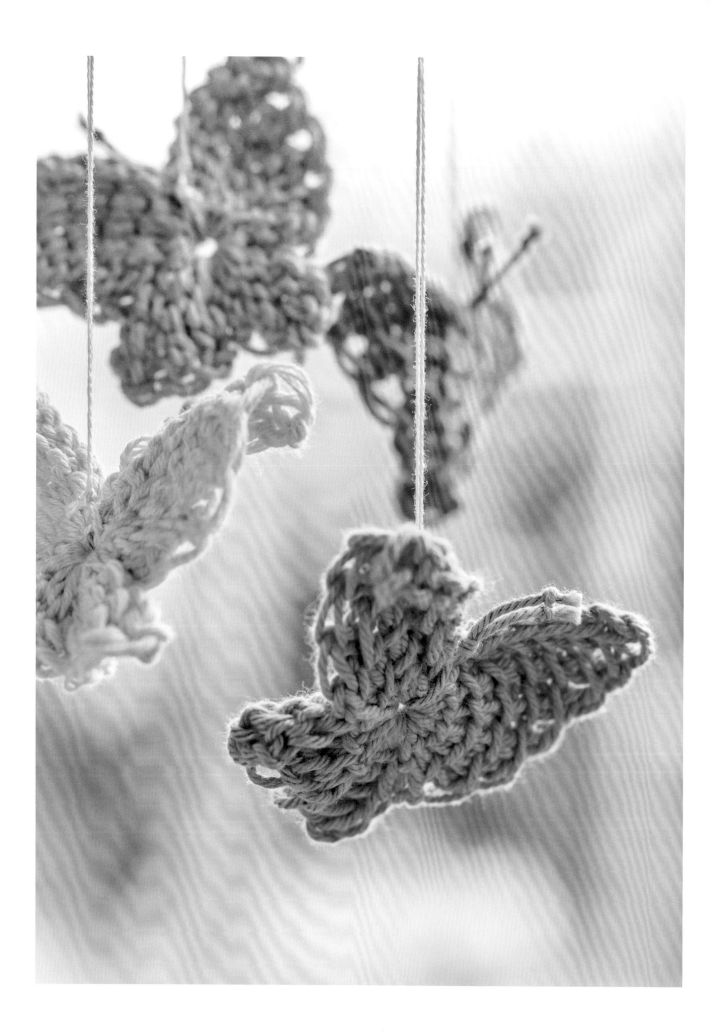

Make it yours

These butterflies use only a very small amount of yarn, so this is an ideal project for you to work with yarns from your stash. To ensure that the butterflies are a consistent size be sure to select yarns of the same weight throughout.

SMALL WING 2

Foundation chain and forward pass: Ch3, starting in second ch from hook, working into back bumps of chain, pick up 2 sts for foundation row. (*3 loops on hook, 3 sts*) Sl st into magic ring continuing counterclockwise around the ring from the last sl st.

Return pass: Yoh, draw through first st, *yoh, draw through next 2 sts on hook; rep from * to end. (*1 st on hook*)

Row 1: M1TSS, TSS to end, sl st into magic ring. (*4 sts*) Work Return Pass.

Row 2: M1TSS, TSS to end, sl st into magic ring. (*5 sts*) Work Return Pass.

Bind (cast) off, don't cut yarn.

LARGE WING 2

Foundation chain and forward pass: Ch3, starting in second ch from hook, working into back bumps of chain, pick up 2 sts for foundation row. (*3 loops on hook, 3 sts*) Sl st into the magic ring continuing counterclockwise around the ring from the last sl st.

Return pass: Yoh, draw through first st, *yoh, draw through next 2 sts on hook; rep from * to end. (*1 st on hook*)

Row 1: M1TSS, TSS to end, sl st into magic ring. (*4 sts*) Work Return Pass.

Row 2: M1TSS, TSS to end, sl st into magic ring. (*5 sts*) Work Return Pass.

Row 3: M1TSS, TSS to end, sl st into magic ring. (*6 sts*) Work Return Pass.

Row 4: M1TSS, TSS to end, sl st into magic ring. (*7 sts*) Work Return Pass.

Row 5: M1TSS, TSS to end, sl st into magic ring. (*8 sts*) Work Return Pass.

Bind (cast) off.

Draw up yarn end to tighten magic ring and make butterfly and fasten off.

Making up and finishing

Weave in all ends of yarn on the butterflies (see page 28). Cut a small length of gray yarn and place a knot at each end. Feed through the upper part of the magic ring and knot to secure to make the antennae.

Prepare the mobile ring by neatly wrapping in ribbon or cotton tape as desired, secure in place with fabric glue. Using the thread, cut four lengths around 15in (38cm) and lay out to create eight spokes around the ring with the threads intersecting at the center to create a star. Place the mobile ring on top of the star. Knot the threads at the side of the ring before passing up and knotting all together at the center top. Thread on some beads above the knot and, if you like, add in the ribbon hanging loop. With the thread held double in the needle, secure it onto the back of a butterfly, and then fasten into place around the mobile with a secure knot. Repeat for each butterfly. Work with varying lengths of thread to allow the butterflies to hang elegantly.

Chapter 3

Pillows & Blankets

Diagonal Baby Blanket

This blanket is quick and fun to make; it's worked from the corner, increasing at each end of the row until the blanket is the desired width, before reversing the process and decreasing back to create the opposite corner.

SKILL RATING: ●

YARN AND MATERIALS

Sirdar Hayfield Spirit Chunky
(80% acrylic, 20% wool) bulky (chunky)
weight, approx 169yd (155m) per
3½oz (100g) ball
   6 balls of Sundown shade 408

HOOK AND EQUIPMENT

US size L-11 (8mm) Tunisian
crochet hook

Yarn needle

FINISHED MEASUREMENTS

37¾ x 37¾in (96 x 96cm)

GAUGE (TENSION)

11 sts x 10 rows = 4 x 4in (10 x 10cm)
in Tunisian Simple Stitch using an US
size L-11 (8mm) hook, after blocking.

ABBREVIATIONS

See page 31.

STITCHES USED

Make 1 (M1TSS) (see page 20)

Tunisian Simple Stitch (TSS)
(see page 14)

Tunisian Simple Stitch 2 together
(2TSStog) (see page 18)

Tunisian Simple Stitch 3 together
(3TSStog) (see page 19)

Blanket

Foundation chain and forward pass: Ch3, starting in second ch from hook, working into back bumps of chain, pick up 2 sts for foundation row. (*3 loops on hook, 3 sts*)
Return pass: Yoh, draw through first st, *yoh, draw through next 2 sts on hook; rep from * to end. (*1 st on hook*)
Increase row: Working into the first space between vertical bars, M1TSS, TSS to last vertical bar, M1TSS in space before last vertical bar, work end st. (*5 sts*)
Work Return Pass.
Rep Increase Row and the Return Pass until there are 145 sts on last Forward Pass, then 1 st on the last Return Pass.
Decrease row: Starting in the second st, 2TSStog, TSS to last 3 vertical bars, 2TSStog, work end st. (*143 sts*)
Work Return Pass.
Rep Decrease Row and the Return Pass until there are 5 sts on hook on the last Forward Pass, then 1 st on the Return Pass.
Last decrease row: Starting in the second st, 3TSStog, work end st. (*3 sts*)
Work Return Pass.
On next Forward Pass row, bind (cast) off.

Making up and finishing

Weave in all ends and block to the desired measurements (see page 28).

TIP This is a great project for stash-busting because you can use this design and work to any size. If you are working from yarn in your stash, simply divide the yarn amount in half—once one half of the yarn is used on the increase rows you can begin the decrease rows.

Join-As-You-Go Patchwork Blanket

This colorful patchwork blanket is ideal for using up all your odds and ends of colorful yarn. Each square is joined in turn, meaning that you can make the blanket any size you like.

SKILL RATING: ●

YARN AND MATERIALS

Stylecraft Special DK (100% acrylic) light worsted (DK) weight yarn, approx 323yd (295m) per 3½oz (100g) ball
   Each square requires approx ¼oz (7g) in a selection of colors

HOOK AND EQUIPMENT

US size J-10 (6mm) Tunisian crochet hook

Yarn needle

FINISHED MEASUREMENTS

39 x 45in (99 x 114cm) with 8 squares wide by 10 squares tall

GAUGE (TENSION)

Each square measures approx 4¼in (10.5cm) square.

ABBREVIATIONS

See page 31.

STITCH USED

Tunisian Simple Stitch (TSS) (see page 14)

Single crochet (sc) (see page 27)

Foundation square

(forms bottom left of blanket)

Foundation chain and forward pass: Ch17, starting in second ch from hook, working into back bumps of chain, pick up 16 sts for foundation row. (*17 loops on hook, 17 sts*)

Return pass: Yoh, draw through first st, *yoh, draw through next 2 sts on hook; rep from * to end. (*1 st on hook*)

Row 1: Starting in the second st, TSS in each st to last vertical bar, work end st. (*17 sts*)
Work Return Pass.

Rows 2–12: Rep Row 1 and the Return Pass. On next Forward Pass row, bind (cast) off.

Upper square

(for every square worked in first column)

Foundation chain and forward pass: Join in new yarn and working along bound- (cast-) off edge, pick up 17 loops for foundation row. (*17 loops on hook, 17 sts*)

Return pass: Yoh, draw through first st, *yoh, draw through next 2 sts on hook; rep from * to end. (*1 st on hook*)

Row 1: Starting in second st, TSS in each st to last vertical bar, work end st. (*17 sts*)
Work Return Pass.

Rows 2–12: Rep Row 1 and the Return Pass. On next Forward Pass row, bind (cast) off.

· ·

Make it yours

Each of the squares in this blanket can be joined in as you go, making this the perfect stash buster. Ensure you select yarns of a similar weight to get an even finish to the squares. You can even return to the blanket at a later date and add in more squares when you have stash yarn to use up!

· ·

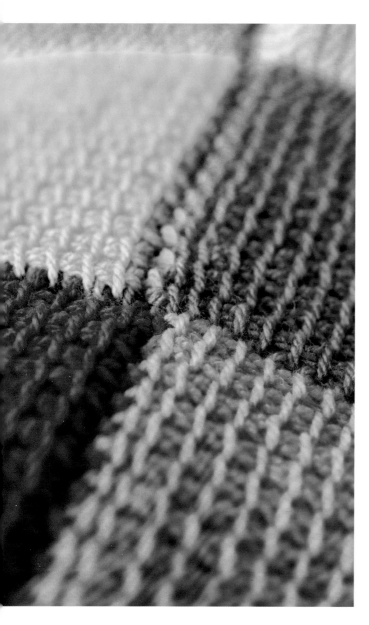

Lower square

(for every base square worked for each subsequent column)

Foundation chain and forward pass: Join in new yarn at corner st on previous left-hand square, ch17, starting in second ch from hook, working into back bumps of chain, pick up 16 sts for foundation row. (*17 loops on hook, 17 sts*)

Return pass: Sl st through end st in square in left-hand panel, *yoh, draw through next 2 sts on hook; rep to end. (*1 st on hook*)

Row 1: Starting in second st, TSS in each st to last vertical bar, work end st. (*17 sts*)
Work Return Pass.

Rows 2–12: Rep Row 1 and the Return Pass.
On next Forward Pass row, bind (cast) off.

Upper square

(for every square worked from a base square after first column)

Foundation chain and forward pass: Join in new yarn and working along bound- (cast-) off edge, pick up 17 loops for foundation row. (*17 loops on hook, 17 sts*)

Return pass: Sl st through end st in block in left-hand panel, *yoh, draw through next 2 sts on hook; rep to end. (*1 st on hook*)

Row 1: Starting in second st, TSS in each st to last vertical bar, work end st. (*17 sts*)
Work Return Pass.

Rows 2–12: Rep Row 1 and the Return Pass.
On next Forward Pass row, bind (cast) off.
Cont adding squares in rows and columns to achieve desired size.

Border

Round 1: Join selected yarn to first st on one side, *1sc in each st to corner, 2sc in corner, 1sc in each row end to corner, 2sc in corner; rep from * to end, sl st to first st to join.

Round 2: Ch1, 1sc in each st to corner, 2sc in corner; rep from * to end, sl st to first st to join.
Fasten off.

Making up and finishing

Weave in all ends and block flat to the desired measurements (see page 28).

Brick Stitch Blanket

This geometric brick-style pattern is surprisingly easy to create, and working with a variegated yarn really makes the stitch pattern stand out.

SKILL RATING: ●●

YARN AND MATERIALS

Lion Brand Babysoft (60% acrylic, 40% nylon) light worsted (DK) weight yarn, approx 459yd (420m) per 5oz (140g) ball
  2 balls of White shade 100 (A)

Lion Brand Mandala Baby (100% acrylic) light worsted (DK) weight, approx 590yd (540m) per 5¼oz (150g) ball
  2 balls of Honey Dukes shade 207AK (B)

HOOK AND EQUIPMENT

US size I-9 (5.5mm) Tunisian crochet hook with cable

Yarn needle

FINISHED MEASUREMENTS

42 x 48in (107 x 122cm)

GAUGE (TENSION)

15 sts x 12 rows = 4 x 4in (10 x 10cm) in Tunisian Brick Stitch using a US size I-9 (5.5mm) hook, after blocking.

ABBREVIATIONS

See page 31.

STITCHES USED

Tunisian Simple Stitch (TSS) (see page 14)

Tunisian Front Post Treble Crochet (TFPTC) (see page 21)

Blanket

Foundation chain and forward pass: Using A, ch161, starting in second ch from hook, working into back bumps of ch, pick up 160 sts for foundation row. (*161 loops on hook, 161 sts*)

Return pass: Yoh, draw through first st, *yoh, draw through next 2 sts on hook; rep from * to end, change to B on yoh of last st on return pass. (*1 st on hook*)

Row 2: Cont in B, starting in second st, TSS in each st to last vertical bar, work end st.
Work Return Pass, changing to A on yoh of last st.

Row 3: Cont in A, starting in second st, *TSS in next 3 sts, TFPTC in next st 2 rows below, miss TSS behind this st; rep from * to last 4 sts, TSS in next 3 sts, work end st.
Work Return Pass, changing to B on yoh of last st.

Row 4: Cont in B, starting in second st, TSS in each st to last vertical bar, work end st.
Work Return Pass, changing to A on yoh of last st.

Row 5: Cont in A, starting in second st, TSS in next st, TFPTC in next st 2 rows below, miss TSS behind this st, *TSS in next 3 sts, TFPTC in next st 2 rows below, miss TSS behind this st; rep from * to last 2 sts, TSS in next st, work end st.
Work Return Pass, changing to B on yoh of last st.
Rows 2–5 create pattern repeat. Cont in pattern as set until work measures 48in (122cm) ending with a row in A. On next Forward Pass row, bind (cast) off using A.

Making up and finishing

Weave in all ends and block flat to the desired measurements (see page 28).

TIPS This blanket was worked using only a selection of the colors from the yarn cake—you can change the look of a blanket by using all or only part of the yarn shades in a yarn cake or ball.

While there are lots of yarn changes on this project, they are all worked on the end of the return pass so there is no need to cut yarn—meaning there are fewer ends to weave in.

Entrelac Pillow

Working back and forth on a small section of stitches at a time creates this clever woven technique. This little pillow is a great starter project to build your skills with entrelac.

SKILL RATING: ● ● ●

YARN AND MATERIALS

Cascade 220 (100% Peruvian wool) worsted (Aran) weight yarn, approx 220yd (200m) per 3½oz (100g) skein (hank)
  1 skein each of:
  Goldenrod shade 7827 (yellow) (A)
  Raspberry Coulis shade 1075 (purple) (B)
  Bristol Blue shade 1004 (turquoise blue) (C)

Toy fiberfill

HOOK AND EQUIPMENT

US size L-11 (8mm) Tunisian crochet hook

Yarn needle

FINISHED MEASUREMENTS

12in (30cm) square

GAUGE (TENSION)

Each small diamond = approx. 1½in (4cm) in Tunisian Simple Stitch using an US size L-11 (8mm) hook, after blocking.

ABBREVIATIONS

See page 31.

STITCHES USED

Tunisian Simple Stitch (TSS) (see page 14)

Single crochet (sc) (see page 27)

Panel

(make 2)

Foundation chain and forward pass: Using A, ch45.

DIAMOND ROW 1

Row 1: Starting in second ch from hook, draw up loops in next 5 ch. (*6 loops on hook*)

Return pass: *Yoh, draw through next 2 sts on hook; rep from * to end. (*1 st on hook*)

Row 2: Starting in second st, TSS in next 4 sts, then pick up loop in next ch. (*6 loops on hook*)
Work Return Pass.

Rows 3 and 4: Rep Row 2 and the Return Pass.

Row 5: Bind (cast) off, sl st bind (cast) off in next ch. (*1 st on hook, 1 diamond made*)

Row 6: Draw up loops in next 5 ch. (*6 loops on hook*)
Work Return Pass.

Rep Rows 2–6 and Return Pass 4 more times.
(*5 diamonds made in total*).

Rep Rows 2–5 once more. (*6 diamonds made in total*)

DIAMOND ROW 2

Row 1: Join B in the first st of the first diamond below, ch1, TSS in next 4 sts in block below, TSS sideways in first st of Row 1 of next block on the left. (*6 loops on hook*)

Return pass: *Yoh, draw through next 2 sts on hook; rep from * to end. (*1 st on hook*)

Row 2: Starting in second st, TSS in next 4 sts in row below, TSS sideways in first st of Row 2 of next block on the left.
Work Return Pass.

TIPS This entrelac technique may look a little daunting, but once the foundation row of diamonds has been worked it is easier to see the placement of subsequent rows of diamonds to work the design.

Note that the Return Pass is worked differently to normal for this project.

Rows 3 and 4: Rep Row 2 and the Return Pass.
Row 5: Bind (cast) off, sl st bind (cast) off in first st of bound- (cast-) off row of next block on the left. (*1 st on hook, 1 diamond made*)
Row 6: Starting in the second st, TSS in next 4 sts in block below, TSS sideways in first st of Row 1 of next block on the left. (*6 loops on hook*)
Work Return Pass.
Rep Rows 2–6 and Return Pass 3 more times.
(*4 diamonds made in total*).
Rep Rows 2–5 once more. (*5 diamonds made in total*)

DIAMOND ROW 3

Join C with a sl st in st at lowest right-hand corner st of previous Diamond Row, ch5.
Row 1: Starting in second ch from hook, draw up loops in next 4ch, draw up 1 loop in same place as sl st. (*6 loops on hook*)
Return pass: *Yoh, draw through next 2 sts on hook; rep from * to end. (*1 st on hook*)
Row 2: Starting in second st, TSS in next 4 sts in row below, TSS sideways in first st of Row 2 of next block on the left.
Work Return Pass.
Rows 3 and 4: Rep Row 2 and the Return Pass.
Row 5: Bind (cast) off, sl st bind (cast) off in first st of bound- (cast-) off row of next block on the left. (*1 st on hook, 1 diamond made*)
Row 6: Starting in the second st, TSS in next 4 sts in block below, TSS sideways in first st of Row 1 of next block on left. (*6 loops on hook*)
Work Return Pass.
Rep Rows 2–6 and Return Pass 3 more times.
(*4 diamonds made in total*)
Rep Rows 2–5 once more. (*5 diamonds made in total*)

FINAL DIAMOND ON ROW 3

Row 1: Starting in second st, TSS in next 3 sts in row below, 2TSS in next st. (*6 loops on hook*)
Return pass: *Yoh, draw through next 2 sts on hook; rep from * to end. (*1 st on hook*)
Row 2: Starting in second st, TSS in next 4 sts in row below, work end st in last st.
Work Return Pass.
Rows 3 and 4: Rep Row 2 and the Return Pass.
Row 5: Bind (cast) off, fasten off last st. (*6 diamonds made in total*)
Rep Diamond Rows 2 and 3 four more times following color sequence of A, B and C, ending on B.

Making up and finishing

Weave in all ends and block flat to the desired measurements (see page 28).
Place the two panels WS together and join A. Work around the outer edge of the pillow with 1sc in each stitch and row edge to join. After two sides have been worked begin filling with toy fiberfill until firm. Work final two sides and fasten off.
Weave in all yarn ends.

Miter Square Pillow

Miter squares are created with carefully placed decreases—once mastered this technique is great for pillows, blankets, wraps, and more!

SKILL RATING: ●●

YARN AND MATERIALS

Cascade Heritage Solids (75% merino wool, 25% nylon) sport (4ply) weight yarn, approx 437yd (400m) per 3½oz (100g) skein (hank)
   1 skein each of:
   Limestone shade 5681 (light gray) (A)
   Clear Sky shade 5781 (light blue) (B)
   Dusty Turquoise shade 5704 (turquoise) (C)
   Deep Ocean shade 5753 (dark green) (D)
   Living Coral shade 5750 (red-orange) (E)
   Golden Yellow shade 5752 (dark yellow) (F)
   Mango shade 5641 (light orange) (G)

10in (25cm) pillow form

3 buttons

HOOK AND EQUIPMENT

US size H-8 (5mm) Tunisian crochet hook

Yarn needle

Locking stitch marker (optional)

Pins

FINISHED MEASUREMENTS

10in (25cm) square

GAUGE (TENSION)

21 sts x 20 rows = 4 x 4in (10 x 10cm) in Tunisian Simple Stitch using a US size H-8 (5mm) hook, after blocking.

ABBREVIATIONS

See page 31.

STITCHES USED

Tunisian Simple Stitch (TSS) (see page 14)

Tunisian Simple Stitch 2 together (2TSStog) (see page 18)

Tunisian Simple Stitch 3 together (3TSStog) (see page 19)

Single crochet (sc) (see page 27)

TIP A locking stitch marker is useful to help you keep track of the center stitch where the decreases need to be worked.

Square

(make 3 in A, 1 in each of B, C, D, E, F, G)
Foundation chain and forward pass: Ch31, starting in second ch from hook, working into back bumps of chain, pick up 30 sts for foundation row.
(*31 loops on hook, 31 sts*)
Return pass: Yoh, draw through first st, *yoh, draw through next 2 sts on hook; rep from * to end. (*1 st on hook*)
PM in center st.
Row 1: Starting in second st, TSS in next 13 sts (14 loops on hook), 3TSStog, TSS in next 13 sts, work end st. (*29 sts*)
Work Return Pass.
Row 2: Starting in second st, TSS in next 12 sts (13 loops on hook), 3TSStog, TSS in next 12 sts, work end st. (*27 sts*)
Work Return Pass.
Row 3: Starting in second st, TSS in next 11 sts (12 loops on hook), 3TSStog, TSS in next 11 sts, work end st. (*25 sts*)
Work Return Pass.
Row 4: Starting in second st, TSS in next 10 sts (11 loops on hook), 3TSStog, TSS in next 10 sts, work end st. (*23 sts*)
Work Return Pass.

Row 5: Starting in second st, TSS in next 9 sts (10 loops on hook), 3TSStog, TSS in next 9 sts, work end st. (*21 sts*)
Work Return Pass.
Row 6: Starting in second st, TSS in next 8 sts (9 loops on hook), 3TSStog, TSS in next 8 sts, work end st. (*19 sts*)
Work Return Pass.
Row 7: Starting in second st, TSS in next 7 sts (8 loops on hook), 3TSStog, TSS in next 7 sts, work end st. (*17 sts*)
Work Return Pass.
Row 8: Starting in second st, TSS in next 6 sts (7 loops on hook), 3TSStog, TSS in next 6 sts, work end st. (*15 sts*)
Work Return Pass.
Row 9: Starting in second st, TSS in next 5 sts (6 loops on hook), 3TSStog, TSS in next 5 sts, work end st. (*13 sts*)
Work Return Pass.
Row 10: Starting in second st, TSS in next 4 sts (5 loops on hook), 3TSStog, TSS in next 4 sts, work end st. (*11 sts*)
Work Return Pass.
Row 11: Starting in second st, TSS in next 3 sts (4 loops on hook), 3TSStog, TSS in next 3 sts, work end st. (*9 sts*)
Work Return Pass.

Row 12: Starting in second st, TSS in next 2 sts (3 loops on hook), 3TSStog, TSS in next 2 sts, work end st. (*7 sts*) Work Return Pass.

Row 13: Starting in second st, TSS in next st (2 loops on hook), 3TSStog, TSS in next st, work end st. (*5 sts*) Work Return Pass.

Row 14: Starting in second st, 3TSStog, work end st. (*3 sts*)

Work Return Pass, thread yarn through 3 remaining sts, ch1, do not break yarn.

BORDER

Round 1: *1sc in each st to corner, 2sc in corner; rep from * to end.
Fasten off.

Pillow back part 1

Foundation chain and forward pass: Using A, ch50, starting in second ch from hook, working into back bumps of chain, pick up 49 sts for foundation row. (*50 loops on hook, 50 sts*)

Return pass: Yoh, draw through first st, *yoh, draw through next 2 sts on hook; rep from * to end. (*1 st on hook*)

Row 1: Starting in second st, TSS in each st to last vertical bar, work end st.
Work Return Pass.
Rep Row 1 and the Return Pass until work measures 6in (15cm).
On next Forward Pass row, bind (cast) off, do not cut yarn.

PILLOW BORDER

Round 1: *1sc in each st to corner, 2sc in corner; rep from * to end.
Fasten off.

Pillow back part 2

Work as Pillow Back Part 1 until work measures 6½in (17cm).

Next row (buttonholes): Starting in second st, TSS in next 9 sts, 2TSStog, TSS in next 12 sts, 2TSStog, TSS in next 12 sts, 2TSStog, TSS in next 9 sts, work end st.

Next 4 rows: Starting in second st, TSS in each st to last vertical bar, work end st.
On next Forward Pass row, bind (cast) off, do not cut yarn.

PILLOW BORDER

Round 1: *1sc in each st to corner, 2sc in corner; rep from * to end.
Fasten off.

Making up and finishing

Weave in all ends and block flat to the desired measurements (see page 28).
Place the miter squares in three rows of three—here the colors have been arranged with two rows of color and a central row of neutral. Once you are happy with the placement, thread a yarn needle with yarn and sew together with mattress stitch (see page 29) to create the pillow front.

FRONT BORDER

Round 1: Join A to first st on one side, *1sc in each st to corner, 2sc in corner; rep from * to end.
Fasten off.

Pin the two back panels onto the pillow front with WS facing and all the side seams aligned. Ensure that the buttonhole panel is outermost. Pin into place. Join A and work *1sc in each st through all layers to corner, 2sc in corner; rep around whole outer edge.
Fasten off and weave in ends.
Sew three buttons onto the back to correspond with the buttonholes (see page 31) and insert pillow form.

Wrap Stitch Blanket

These clusters of stitches are worked by using a yarn over to make an additional loop to wrap the stitches. Made in repeated strips, this colorful blanket works up surprisingly quickly.

SKILL RATING: ● ●

YARN AND MATERIALS

Caron Simply Soft (100% acrylic) worsted (Aran) weight yarn, approx 315yd (288m) per 6oz (170g) ball
   1 ball each of:
   Off White shade 9702 (A)
   Robin's Egg shade 9780 (teal) (B)
   Plum Wine shade 9722 (dark pink) (C)
   Soft Blue shade 9712 (light blue) (D)

HOOK AND EQUIPMENT

US size K-10½ (6.5mm) Tunisian crochet hook

Yarn needle

FINISHED MEASUREMENTS

25½ x 29in (65 x 74cm)

GAUGE (TENSION)

16 sts x 10.5 rows = 4 x 4in (10 x 10cm) in Tunisian Simple Stitch using a US size K-10½ (6.5mm) hook, after blocking.

ABBREVIATIONS

See page 31.

STITCHES USED

Tunisian Simple Stitch (TSS) (see page 14)

Yarn over (YO) (see page 23)

Single crochet (sc) (see page 27)

TIP The wrap stitches are created by bringing the yarn over the hook in a YO and working three stitches before lifting the loop of the YO over the stitches to wrap them. Be sure not to pull the yarn too tight when making the yarn over to keep the gauge (tension) consistent.

Blanket

Foundation chain and forward pass: Using A, ch94, starting in second ch from hook, working into back bumps of ch, pick up 93 sts for foundation row. (*94 loops on hook, 94 sts*)

Return pass: Yoh, draw through first st, *yoh, draw through next 2 sts on hook; rep from * to end. (*1 st on hook*)

Row 1: Starting in second st, TSS to last vertical bar, work end st. (*94 sts*)

Work Return Pass, changing to B on last yoh.

Row 2: Starting in second st, TSS, *YO, TSS in next 3 sts, lift YO round sts to wrap; rep from * to last 2 sts, TSS in last st, work end st.

Work Return Pass.

Rows 3–5: Rep Row 2 and the Return Pass.

Row 6: Starting in second st, TSS, *YO, TSS in next 3 sts, lift YO round sts to wrap; rep from * to last 2 sts, TSS in last st, work end st.

Work Return Pass, changing to A on last yoh.

Row 7: Starting in second st, TSS in each st to last st, work end st.

Work Return Pass, changing to C on last yoh.

Row 8: Starting in second st, TSS, *YO, TSS in next 3 sts, lift YO round sts to wrap; rep from * to last 2 sts, TSS in next st, work end st.

Work Return Pass.

Rows 9–11: Rep Row 8 and the Return Pass.

Row 12: Starting in second st, TSS, *YO, TSS in next 3 sts, lift YO round sts to wrap; rep from * to last 2 sts, TSS in last st, work end st.

Work Return Pass, changing to A on last yoh.

Row 13: Starting in second st, TSS in each st to last st, work end st.

Work Return Pass, changing to D on last yoh.

Row 14: Starting in second st, TSS, *YO, TSS in next 3 sts, lift YO round sts to wrap; rep from * to last 2 sts, TSS in next st, work end st.

Work Return Pass.

Rows 15–17: Rep Row 14 and the Return Pass.

Row 18: Starting in second st, TSS, *YO, TSS in next 3 sts, lift YO round sts to wrap; rep from * to last 2 sts, TSS in last st, work end st.
Work Return Pass, changing to A on last yoh.
Rows 1–18 create color repeat. Repeat these rows 3 more times. leaving yarn A attached after the last row.
Next row: Starting in second st, TSS in each st to last st, work end st.
Next row: Starting in second st, TSS in each st to last st, work end st.
On next Forward Pass row, bind (cast) off.

CROCHET BORDER

Join in A at any corner.
Round 1: Ch1, *2sc in corner, 1sc in each st to next corner; rep from * 3 times, sl st to first st to join.
Rounds 2–4: Rep Round 1.
Round 5: Change to B, rep Round 1.
Round 6: Change to A, rep Round 1.
Fasten off.

Making up and finishing

Weave in all ends and block flat to the desired measurements (see page 28).

Round Pillow

This cozy pillow is created by joining and filling two circular panels. Working in rows from the center to the edges and using short row shaping, this project is a great opportunity to build your skills.

SKILL RATING: ● ●

YARN AND MATERIALS

James C Brett Aurora (80% acrylic, 20% wool) light worsted (DK) weight, approx 377yd (345m) per 3½oz (100g) ball
    1 ball of Stormy Skies shade AU04

HOOK AND EQUIPMENT

US size J-10 (6mm) Tunisian crochet hook

Yarn needle

Locking or split-ring stitch marker

Toy fiberfill

FINISHED MEASUREMENTS

14in (36cm) diameter

GAUGE (TENSION)

12.5 sts x 12 rows = 4 x 4in (10 x 10cm) in Tunisian Simple Stitch using a US size J-10 (6mm) hook.

ABBREVIATIONS

See page 31.

STITCHES USED

Magic ring (see page 26)

Single crochet (sc) (see page 27)

Tunisian Simple Stitch (TSS) (see page 14)

NOTE

This pattern works with standard crochet in the round and Tunisian Crochet.

TIPS If you are using a long Tunisian Crochet hook for your project you may also need a US size J-10 (6mm) standard hook for the single crochet base section, so that the extra length doesn't make it awkward to work the stitches. Alternatively, a Tunisian hook with a cable is very versatile and can be used for smaller and larger elements alike.

To avoid gaps in the rows following the short rows, work into the stitch below after the end of the short row as this will help to draw up the rows together.

Pillow panel

(make 2)

Make a magic ring.

Round 1: 6sc into ring. *(6 sts)*

PM at start of round.

Round 2: [2sc in next st] 6 times. *(12 sts)*

Round 3: [1sc in next st, 2sc in next st] 6 times. *(18 sts)*

Round 4: [1sc in next 2 sts, 2sc in next st] 6 times.
(24 sts)

Begin working in TSS with short row shaping.

Foundation chain and forward pass: Sl st in first st in
foundation circle, ch20, starting in second ch from hook,
working into back bumps of chain, pick up 19 sts for
foundation row. *(20 loops on hook, 20 sts)*

Return pass 1: Sl st in next st in foundation circle, *yoh,
draw through next 2 sts on hook; rep from * to end.
(1 st on hook)

Row 1: Starting in second st, TSS in next 17 sts.
(18 loops on hook, 18 sts)

Return pass 2: Sl st in next TSS st, *yoh, draw through
next 2 sts on hook; rep from * to end. *(1 st on hook)*

Row 2: TSS in next 14 sts. *(15 loops on hook, 15 sts)*
Work Return Pass 2.

Row 3: TSS in next 9 sts. *(10 loops on hook, 10 sts)*
Work Return Pass 2.

Row 4: TSS in next 9 sts, then TSS in 5 sts of row below,
then TSS in 3 sts of row below that, then TSS in last
2 sts of row below that. *(20 loops on hook, 20 sts)*
Work Return Pass 1.

Row 5: Starting in second st, TSS in next 17 sts.
(18 loops on hook, 18 sts)
Work Return Pass 2.

Row 6: TSS in next 14 sts. *(15 loops on hook, 15 sts)*
Work Return Pass 2.

Row 7: TSS in next 9 sts. *(10 loops on hook, 10 sts)*
Work Return Pass 2.

Rep Rows 4–7 and Return Pass as set 22 more times,
then Row 4 once more, ending after a Return Pass with
1 loop on hook.

Join with a sl st and fasten off.

Making up and finishing

Block flat as desired (see page 28).

Align the two long edges and thread a yarn needle
with the yarn tail. Work in mattress stitch (see page 29)
to secure the side seam from the edge of the circle to
the foundation circle.

Fasten off.

Weave in all yarn ends (see page 28).

Place the two pieces together with WS facing and
with yarn and US size J-10 (6mm) hook, work around
the outer edge with 1sc in each row end to join the
pieces together.

Fill with fiberfill until firm before completing the seam
and fastening off.

Chapter 4
Bags & Gifts

Bookmark

Whether you make it for yourself or to give as a gift, this bookmark is a real classic. It's worked in silky soft Perlé cotton, which gives a luxurious luster to the Tunisian Simple Stitches.

SKILL RATING: ●

YARN AND MATERIALS

DMC Cotton Perlé (100% mercerized cotton) Size 3, approx 16yd (15m) per ⅛oz (5g) skein (hank)
1 skein each of:
  Scallion shade 3348 (light green) (A)
  Coral shade 351 (red-orange) (B)

HOOK AND EQUIPMENT

US size D-3 (3mm) Tunisian crochet hook

Yarn needle

Small pieces of card to make tassel

FINISHED MEASUREMENTS

6¾ x 2¼in (17.5 x 5.5cm) excluding tassel

GAUGE (TENSION)

6 sts x 5 rows = 1 x 1in (2.5 x 2.5cm) in Tunisian Simple Stitch using a US size D-3 (3mm) hook, after blocking.

ABBREVIATIONS

See page 131.

STITCHES USED

Tunisian Simple Stitch (TSS) (see page 14)

Single crochet (sc) (see page 27)

Bookmark

Foundation chain and forward pass: Ch12, starting in second ch from hook, working into back bumps of chain, pick up 11 sts for foundation row. (*12 loops on hook, 12 sts*)
Return pass: Yoh, draw through first st, *yoh, draw through next 2 sts on hook; rep to end. (*1 st on hook*)
Row 1 (forward pass): Starting in the second st, TSS to last vertical bar, work end st. (*12 sts*)
Work Return Pass.
Rep Row 1 and the Return Pass, maintaining st count on Forward Pass, until work measures 6¾in (17.5cm) in length.
On next Forward Pass row, bind (cast) off.

Making up and finishing

Fasten off A. Weave in all ends and block flat to the desired measurements (see page 28).
Join in B and work around the outer edge with 1sc in each stitch and 2sc in each of the corner stitches. Slip stitch into first stitch and fasten off.

Cut a strip of card to 2in (5cm) wide. Wrap B around the card 40 times to make tassel. Thread short lengths of B under all the loops at one edge and knot securely. Cut through the loops on the opposite edge to remove the tassel from the card. Tie another short length of B around the strands just below the top to secure and trim the ends to match the tassel strands. Braid the lengths of B at the top of the tassel before securing the ends to the bottom of the bookmark, and knotting in place securely.
Weave in all ends.

TIP This bookmark is made with a lightweight thread rather than a yarn, to allow it to sit neatly in-between the pages of a book. Work with a Perlé or ply cotton, rather than a stranded cotton, to avoid splitting the threads as you work the stitches.

Gadget Sleeve Case

Keep your gadget protected in a custom-fit sleeve. This design is worked in Tunisian Knit Stitch, making it a speedy project—make use of variegated yarns for a colorful design with no extra ends to weave in.

SKILL RATING: ●

YARN AND MATERIALS

Stylecraft Knit Me, Crochet Me (80% acrylic, 20% wool) light worsted (DK) weight, approx 317yd (290m) per 3½oz (100g) ball
   1 ball of Rainbow shade 6151

HOOK AND EQUIPMENT

US size J-10 (6mm) Tunisian crochet hook

Yarn needle

FINISHED MEASUREMENTS

6½ x 5¼in (17 x 13cm) when folded

GAUGE (TENSION)

7.5 sts x 10 rows = 2 x 2in (5 x 5cm) in Tunisian Knit Stitch using a US size J-10 (6mm) hook, after blocking.

ABBREVIATIONS

See page 31.

STITCHES USED

Tunisian Knit Stitch (TKS) (see page 15)

Tunisian Purl Stitch (TPS) (see page 16)

NOTE

The last TPS stitch in the forward pass row will sit slightly differently on the hook so you will need to insert the hook carefully to avoid missing or twisting the stitch—see Techniques: End Stitch (page 14).

· ·

Make it yours

This fits the Kindle Paperwhite 10th Gen, which is 6½ x 4½in (16.7 x 11.6cm), but can be customized by adjusting the amount of stitches that you cast on for the foundation row: more stitches for a wider sleeve and fewer for a narrower sleeve. The length can be adjusted by increasing the portion worked in Tunisian Knit Stitch—hold the piece against the item as you work to get the exact size.

· ·

Sleeve case

Foundation chain and forward pass: Ch20, starting in second ch from hook, working into back bumps of chain, pick up 19 sts for foundation row. (*20 loops on hook, 20 sts*)

Return pass: Yoh, draw through first st, *yoh, draw through next 2 sts on hook; rep from * to end. (*1 st on hook*)

Row 1: Starting in the second st, *TKS, TPS; rep from * to last vertical bar, work end st. (*20 sts*)
Work Return Pass.

Rows 2 and 3: Rep Row 1 and the Return Pass twice more.

Row 4 (forward pass): Starting in the second st, TKS to last vertical bar, work end st. (*20 sts*)
Work Return Pass.
Rep Row 4 and the Return Pass, maintaining st count on Forward Pass, until work measures 11¾in (30cm) from cast-on edge.

Next row 1: Starting in the second st, *TKS, TPS; rep from * to last vertical bar, work end st. (*20 sts*)
Work Return Pass.
Rep Next Row 1 and the Return Pass twice more.
On next Forward Pass row, bind (cast) off.
Leave a long tail to sew together.

Making up and finishing

Weave in all ends and block flat to the desired measurements (see page 28).

Fold the strip in half, aligning the ribbed edges, and thread a yarn needle with the yarn tail. Work in mattress stitch (see page 29) to secure the side seam and then fasten off. Repeat with a second length of yarn to secure the second side.

Fasten off and weave in all yarn ends.

Button-up Purse

This mini pouch is ideal for stowing your make-up essentials, sunglasses or reading spectacles. The super plush crochet will give your glasses some light-padded protection from scuffs and scrapes. This design is worked in Tunisian Simple Stitch, but alternating the yarns at each forward and return pass creates a striking woven finish.

SKILL RATING: ● ●

YARN AND MATERIALS

Berroco Ultra Alpaca (50% super fine alpaca, 50% Peruvian wool) worsted (Aran) weight, approx 219yd (200m) per 3½oz (100g) skein (hank)

    1 skein each of:
    Zephyr shade 62111 (light blue) (A)
    Tea Rose shade 62114 (pink) (B)

Large button

HOOK AND EQUIPMENT

US size K-10½ (6.5mm) Tunisian crochet hook

Yarn needle

Pins

FINISHED MEASUREMENTS

6¾ x 4in (17.5 x 10cm) when seamed and closed

GAUGE (TENSION)

8 sts x 7 rows = 2 x 2in (5 x 5cm) in Tunisian Simple Stitch using a US size K-10½ (6.5mm) hook.

ABBREVIATIONS

See page 31.

STITCH USED

Tunisian Simple Stitch (TSS) (see page 14)

Case

Foundation chain and forward pass: Using A, ch28, starting in second ch from hook, working into back bumps of chain, pick up 27 sts for foundation row. (*28 loops on hook, 28 sts*)

Return pass 1: Yoh, draw through first st, *yoh, draw through next 2 sts on hook; rep from * to end. (*1 st on hook*)

Row 1: Starting in the second st, TSS to last vertical bar, work end st. (*28 sts*)

Return pass 2 (work for this and all subsequent return passes): Change to B, yoh, draw through first st, *yoh, draw through next 2 sts on hook; rep from * to last 2 sts on hook, pick up A, yoh, draw through last 2 sts on hook. (*1 st on hook in A*)

Row 2: Cont in A, starting in the second st, TSS to last vertical bar, work end st. (*28 sts*)

Work Return Pass 2.

Rep Row 2 and the Return Pass 2, alternating yarns on Forward and Return Pass, maintaining st count on Forward Pass, until work measures 9in (23cm) from cast-on edge, ending with a Forward Pass in A.

Final return pass: Cont in A, yoh, draw through first st, *yoh, draw through next 2 sts on hook; rep from * to end. (*1 st on hook*)

On next Forward Pass row, bind (cast) off.

Making up and finishing

Weave in all yarn ends at the color changes and block flat to the desired measurements (see page 28).

With the WS uppermost, fold up 3½in (9cm) at the bottom to form the pouch and pin in place. Using a length of A threaded into a yarn needle, work in running stitch (see page 30) to sew the side seams for both folded lower sections.

Fold down the remaining 1½in (4cm) to make the upper portion and use pins to mark the center front and upper flap for the button and button loop placement. Sew the button securely into place at the center front (see page 31).

Using A, work a ch10 leaving a long tail at the start and end. Thread the tails into a yarn needle and use to secure this button loop to the inside of the upper flap to correspond with the button.

Fasten off and weave in ends.

TIP Alternating the yarns between each forward and return pass will mean that there are lot of ends to sew in. When working the color changes, hold the yarn in place and work a few stitches before securing with knots, as this will help to keep the integrity of the stitch shape.

Wrist Warmers

Wrist warmers are ideal for keeping busy hands cozy—not only do you still have the freedom to use your fingers but the extra insulation also helps keep the blood flowing.

SKILL RATING: ●

YARN AND MATERIALS

Sirdar JewelSpun With Wool Chunky (80% acrylic, 20% wool) bulky (chunky) weight, approx 328yd (300m) per 7oz (200g) ball
   1 ball of Mother of Pearl shade 203

HOOK AND EQUIPMENT

US size L-11 (8mm) Tunisian crochet hook

Yarn needle

FINISHED MEASUREMENTS

7 x 3¾in (18 x 9.5cm) when laid flat

GAUGE (TENSION)

6 sts x 5 rows = 2 x 2in (5 x 5cm) in Tunisian Simple Stitch using an US size L-11 (8mm) hook, after blocking.

ABBREVIATIONS

See page 31.

STITCHES USED

Tunisian Knit Stitch (TKS) (see page 15)

Tunisian Purl Stitch (TPS) (see page 16)

Tunisian Simple Stitch (TSS) (see page 14)

NOTE

The last TPS stitch in the forward pass row will sit slightly differently on the hook so you will need to insert the hook carefully to avoid missing or twisting the stitch—see Techniques: End stitch (page 14)

• •

Make it yours

When worked in a chunky yarn these wrist warmers are super warm. However, if you would prefer a more dainty finish you can work with a light worsted (DK) yarn—but remember you will need to increase the number of stitches and rows worked and you will need to match your hook size to suit your yarn.

• •

Wrist warmer

(make 2)

Foundation chain and forward pass: Ch22, starting in second ch from hook, working into back bumps of chain, pick up 21 sts for foundation row. (*22 loops on hook, 22 sts*)

Return pass: Yoh, draw through first st, *yoh, draw through next 2 sts on hook; rep from * to end. (*1 st on hook*)

Row 1: Starting in the second st, *TKS, TPS; rep from * to last vertical bar, work end st. (*22 sts*)
Work Return Pass.

Rows 2–4: Rep Row 1 and the Return Pass 3 more times.

Row 5: Starting in the second st, TSS to last vertical bar, work end st. (*22 sts*)
Work Return Pass.
Rep Row 5 and the Return Pass, maintaining st count on Forward Pass, for 10 rows or until work measures 15.5cm (6in) from cast-on edge.

Next row: Starting in the second st, *TKS, TPS; rep from * to last vertical bar, work end st. (*20 sts*)
Work Return Pass.
Rep Next Row above and the Return Pass 3 more times.
On next Forward Pass row, bind (cast) off.
Leave a long tail to sew together.

Making up and finishing

Weave in all ends and block flat to the desired measurements (see page 28).
Fold the strip in half, aligning the long edges, and thread a yarn needle with the yarn tail. Work in mattress stitch (see page 29) to secure the side seam for 1½in (4cm) from the top and then fasten off.
Rejoin the yarn and create a second seam working from the bottom section of ribbing upward for 4in (10cm), then fasten off. This leaves an opening in the seam for the thumb.
Repeat with the second wrist warmer.
Fasten off and weave in all yarn ends.

Tote Bag

Whether you're heading to the library or farmers' market, this roomy tote bag will stow all your essentials. Created with a combination of crochet and Tunisian crochet and finished with leather-style straps, this bag is a timeless classic.

SKILL RATING: ●

YARN AND MATERIALS

Hoooked Ribbon XL Solid (80% cotton, 20% other) bulky (chunky) weight, approx 131yd (120m) per 8¾oz (250g) ball
1 ball in each of:
   Spicy Ocre (green) (A)
   Sandy Ecru (off-white) (B)

Leather-style bag straps

Small pieces of Mylar®/plastic canvas (optional)

HOOK AND EQUIPMENT

US size P-16/Q (12mm) Tunisian crochet hook

Yarn needle

Locking or split-ring stitch marker

FINISHED MEASUREMENTS

Base: 11½in (29cm) long x 4½in (11.5cm) wide

Height: 8¾in (22cm)

GAUGE (TENSION)

10 sts x 7.5 rows = 4 x 4in (10 x 10cm) in Tunisian Simple Stitch using a US size P-16/Q (12mm) hook.

ABBREVIATIONS

See page 31.

STITCHES USED

Single crochet (sc) (see page 27)

Tunisian Simple Stitch (TSS) (see page 14)

NOTE

This pattern works with standard crochet and Tunisian Crochet.

Base

Using A, ch15.

Round 1: 1sc in second ch from hook, 1sc in each ch to last ch, PM, 3sc in last ch, turn work and cont working on opp side, 1sc in each ch to last ch, PM, 3sc in last ch, sl st to join. (*32 sts*)

PM at start of round.

Round 2: Ch1, 1sc in each st to first marker, 2sc in next 3 sts, 1sc in each st to second marker, 2sc in next 3 sts, sl st to join. (*38 sts*)

Round 3: Ch1, 1sc in each st to first marker, [2sc in next st, 1sc] 3 times, 1sc in each st to second marker, [2sc in next st, 1sc] 3 times, sl st to join. (*44 sts*)

Round 4: Ch1, 1sc in each st to first marker, [2sc in next st, 2sc] 3 times, 1sc in each st to second marker, [2sc in next st, 2sc] 3 times, sl st to join. (*50 sts*)

Round 5: Ch1, 1sc in each st to first marker, [2sc in next st, 3sc] 3 times, 1sc in each st to second marker, [2sc in next st, 3sc] 3 times, sl st to join. (*56 sts*)

Round 6: 1scBLO in each st, continue in a spiral without joining. (*56 sts*)

Rounds 7–10: 1sc in each st. (*56 sts*)

Sl st into first st and fasten off A.

Sides

Begin working in Tunisian Simple Stitch.

Foundation chain and forward pass: Using B, ch8, starting in second ch from hook, working into back bumps of chain, pick up 7 sts for foundation row. (*8 loops on hook, 8 sts*)

Return pass: Pass hook through BLO of next st of crochet circle base, yoh and draw through, bring through first st, *yoh, draw through next 2 sts on hook; rep from * to end.

Row 1: Starting in second st, TSS to last vertical bar, work end st. (*8 sts*)

Work Return Pass.

Rep Row 1 and return pass 53 more times.

On next Forward Pass row, bind (cast) off in TSS.

Making up and finishing

Align the two straight edges and thread a yarn needle with the yarn tail. Work in mattress stitch (see page 29) to secure the back seam of the bag.

Fasten off.

Weave in all yarn ends (see page 28).

Place the bag handles into position and secure following the manufacturer's instructions—inserting a piece of Mylar® or plastic canvas at the inside to anchor the handles (optional).

TIPS If you are using a long Tunisian Crochet hook for your project you may also need a US size P-16/Q (12mm) standard hook for the single crochet base section, so that the extra length doesn't make it awkward to work the stitches. Alternatively, a Tunisian hook with a cable is pretty versatile and can be used for smaller and larger elements alike.

The base section of this bag is worked in crochet in the round; using a locking or split-ring stitch marker will help you to identify the start of each round. Sl st at the end of each round to join. Slip each marker as you come to it.

When fixing bag handles to crochet bags you may like to cut a piece of Mylar® or plastic canvas to place onto the inside of the bag at the handle position. This plastic will help to anchor the straps in place and prevent the fastenings from being pulled through the crochet fabric.

Zipper Coin Purse

Stand out from the crowd with this lightning bolt motif zipper purse, worked with alternating yarns for a bold striped background.

SKILL RATING: ●

YARN AND MATERIALS

DMC Baby Cotton (100% cotton) light worsted (DK) weight, approx 116yd (106m) per 1¾oz (50g) ball

1 ball each of:
  Royal Blue shade 798 (A)
  White shade 762 (B)

Small amounts of cotton light worsted (DK) in each of:
  Yellow (C)
  Pink (D)
  Turquoise (E)

6¼in (16cm) closed end zipper

HOOKS AND EQUIPMENT

US size I-9 (5.5mm) Tunisian crochet hook

US size D-3 (3.25mm) standard crochet hook

Yarn needle

Sewing thread and needle

Pins

FINISHED MEASUREMENTS

7 x 4¼in (18 x 11cm)

GAUGE (TENSION)

14 sts x 15 rows = 4 x 4in (10 x 10cm) in Tunisian Simple Stitch using a US size I-9 (5.5mm) hook.

ABBREVIATIONS

See page 31.

STITCHES USED

Tunisian Simple Stitch (TSS) (see page 14)

Motif is created using single crochet (sc) (see page 27)

Coin purse

Foundation chain and forward pass: Using 5.5mm (US size I-9) Tunisian crochet hook and A, ch26, starting in second ch from hook, working into back bumps of chain, pick up 25 sts for foundation row. (*26 loops on hook, 26 sts*)

Return pass: Yoh, draw through first st, *yoh, draw through next 2 sts on hook; rep from * to end. (*1 st on hook*)

Row 1: Starting in second st, TSS in each st to last vertical bar, work end st. (*26 sts*)
Work Return Pass.

Row 2: Change to B, starting in second st, TSS in each st to last vertical bar, work end st. (*26 sts*)
Work Return Pass.

Rep Row 1 and Return Pass in A, then Row 2 and Return Pass in B, 14 more times.

Next row: Change to A, starting in second st, TSS in each st to last vertical bar, work end st. (*26 sts*)
Work Return Pass.

On next Forward Pass row, bind (cast) off in TSS using A.

TIP When sewing the motif onto the front of the coin purse, be sure that you are only sewing through the top layer and not through both layers.

Lightning bolt motif

Using US size D-3 (3.25mm) crochet hook and C, ch2.
Row 1: 1sc in second ch from hook, turn. (*1 st*)
Row 2: Ch1 (counts as turning ch throughout), 2sc in first st, turn. (*2 sts*)
Row 3: Ch1, 1sc in each st to end, turn.
Row 4: Ch1, 2sc in next st, 1sc in next st, turn. (*3 sts*)
Row 5: Ch1, 1sc in each st to end, turn.
Row 6: Ch1, 2sc in next st, 1sc in next 2 sts, turn. (*4 sts*)
Row 7: Ch1, 1sc in each st to end, turn.
Row 8: Ch1, 2sc in next st, 1sc in next 3 sts, turn. (*5 sts*)
Row 9: Ch1, 1sc in each st to end, turn.
Row 10: Ch1, 2sc in next st, 1sc in next 4 sts, ch4, turn. (*6 sts, ch-4*)
Row 11: Starting in second ch from hook, 1sc in next 3 sts of ch, 1sc in next 3 sts of project, turn. (*6 sts*)
Row 12: Ch1, 2sc in next st, 1sc in next 3 sts, sc2tog, turn.
Row 13: Ch1, 1sc in each st to end, turn.
Row 14: Ch1, 2sc in next st, 1sc in next 3 sts, sc2tog, turn.
Row 15: Ch1, 1sc in each st to end, turn.
Row 16: Ch1, 2sc in next st, 1sc in next 3 sts, sc2tog, turn.
Row 17: Ch1, 1sc in each st to end, turn.
Fasten off.

Making up and finishing

Weave in all ends and block flat to the desired measurements (see page 28).
Fold the coin purse in half, aligning the edges. Using a US size I-9 (5.5mm) crochet hook, join in A at the bottom edge and work each side seam in turn with 1sc in each stitch to join, fasten off.
Pin the motif onto the front. Thread a yarn needle with C. Sew into place on the front securely with running stitch.
Using D, sew accents along one side using long stitches.
Open the zipper and pin into place along the upper section of the coin purse. Working with the sewing cotton and needle, sew each of the zipper tabs into place using small neat stitches.
Finish wth a tassel on the zipper tab by cutting 4¼in (10.5cm) lengths of E and passing through the tab, then secure into place with a length of E knotted around near the top.

Snap Frame Purse

The dense finished fabric of Tunisian Simple Stitch is great for bags and purses. A metallic yarn really elevates this simple design for a deluxe finish.

SKILL RATING: ● ●

YARN AND MATERIALS

Rico Fashion Cotton Métallisé DK (53% cotton, 35% acrylic, 12% metallic fibers) light worsted (DK) weight yarn, approx 142yd (130m) per 1¾oz (50g) ball
  1 ball of Gold shade 03

8in (20cm) snap closing purse frame

Fabric glue (optional)

HOOK AND EQUIPMENT

US size J-10 (6mm) Tunisian crochet hook

Yarn needle

FINISHED MEASUREMENTS

8 x 6¼in (20 x 16cm) including frame

GAUGE (TENSION)

15 sts x 13 rows = 4 x 4in (10 x 10cm) in Tunisian Simple Stitch using a US size J-10 (6mm) hook, after blocking.

ABBREVIATIONS

See page 31.

STITCH USED

Tunisian Simple Stitch (TSS) (see page 14)

Purse

Foundation chain and forward pass: Ch25, starting in second ch from hook, working into back bumps of chain, pick up 24 sts for foundation row. (*25 loops on hook, 25 sts*)

Return pass: Yoh, draw through first st, *yoh, draw through next 2 sts on hook; rep from * to end. (*1 st on hook*)

Row 1: Starting in second st, TSS in each st to end, work end st.

Work Return Pass.

Rows 2–40: Rep Row 1 and the Return Pass.
On next Forward Pass row, bind (cast) off.

Bow accent (large piece)

Foundation chain and forward pass: Ch12, starting in second ch from hook, working into back bumps of chain, pick up 11 sts for foundation row. (*12 loops on hook, 12 sts*)

Return pass: Yoh, draw through first st, *yoh, draw through next 2 sts on hook; rep from * to end. (*1 st on hook*)

Row 1: Starting in second st, TSS in each st to end, work end st.

Work Return Pass.

Rows 2–18: Rep Row 1 and the Return Pass.
On next Forward Pass row, bind (cast) off.

Bow center (smaller piece)

Foundation chain and forward pass: Ch4, starting in second ch from hook, working into back bumps of chain, pick up 3 sts for foundation row. (*4 loops on hook, 4 sts*)

Return pass: Yoh, draw through first st, *yoh, draw through next 2 sts on hook; rep from * to end. (*1 st on hook*)

Row 1: Starting in the second st, TSS in each st to end. work end st. (*4 sts*)

Work Return Pass.

Rows 2–8: Rep Row 1 and the Return Pass.
On next Forward Pass row, bind (cast) off.

Making up and finishing

Weave in all ends and block flat to the desired measurements (see page 28).

Fold the purse section in half aligning the two shorter ends. Position into the frame and secure as per the manufacturer's instructions. Add fabric glue to secure if desired.

Thread a yarn needle with yarn and work each side in turn to sew the side seams from the folded lower edge to the base of the purse frame using running stitch (see page 30).

Place the smaller Bow Center piece into the center of the larger Bow Accent piece and wrap around the center drawing up the middle of the bow. Thread a yarn needle with yarn and sew in place with a couple of stitches before securing to the purse.

Open the purse and place the bow onto the center front, using the yarn to sew in place securely.

Fasten off and weave in all yarn ends.

Suppliers

USA

LoveCrafts
Yarns, Tunisian crochet hooks,
craft supplies
Online sales
www.lovecrafts.com

Knitting Fever Inc.
Yarns, craft supplies
www.knittingfever.com

WEBS
Yarns, Tunisian crochet hooks,
craft supplies
www.yarn.com

Jo-Ann Fabric and Craft Stores
Yarns and craft supplies
www.joann.com

Michaels
Yarns, Tunisian crochet hooks,
craft supplies
www.michaels.com

UK

LoveCrafts
Yarns, Tunisian crochet hooks,
craft supplies
Online sales
www.lovecrafts.com

Wool
Yarns
Store in Bath
+44 (0)1225 469144
www.woolbath.co.uk

Wool Warehouse
Yarns, Tunisian crochet hooks,
craft supplies
Online sales
www.woolwarehouse.co.uk

Laughing Hens
Yarns, Tunisian crochet hooks,
craft supplies
Tel: +44 (0) 1829 740903
www.laughinghens.com

John Lewis
Yarns and craft supplies
Telephone numbers of stores
on website
www.johnlewis.com

Hobbycraft
Yarns and craft supplies
www.hobbycraft.co.uk

Australia

Black Sheep Wool 'n' Wares
Yarns and craft supplies
Retail store and online
Tel: +61 (0)2 6779 1196
www.blacksheepwool.com.au

Sun Spun
Yarns and craft supplies
Retail store (Canterbury, Victoria)
and online
Tel: +61 (0)3 9830 1609
www.sunspun.com.au

If you wish to substitute a different
yarn for the one recommended in the
pattern, try the Yarnsub website for
suggestions: www.yarnsub.com

Index

Acknowledgments

Firstly, I'd love to thank all the makers and crafters who have supported my creative journey over the years.

Thank you also to the tremendous and talented team at CICO Books.

Finally, I want to express my gratitude to my husband, John, and our family for their endless support and encouragement.